cognitive behavioral therapy & mindfulness toolbox

50 Tips, Tools and Handouts for Anxiety, Stress, Depression, Personality & Mood Disorders

Richard Sears, PsyD, PhD, MBA, ABPP

Copyright © 2017 by Richard Sears

Published by:

PESI Publishing & Media
PESI, Inc.
3839 White Ave
Eau Claire, WI 54703

Cover: Amy Rubenzer
Editing: Donald Altman
Layout: Bookmasters & Amy Rubenzer

Proudly printed in the United States

ISBN: 9781683730682

PESI
Publishing
& Media
www.pesipublishing.com

Endorsements

"Richard Sears is that rare psychologist and mindfulness trainer who brings decades of authentic training in classical meditation methods into contact with the razor's edge of our most recent research developments. Having a chance to train with Richard is a gift, and this book is like your own private session of advanced mindfulness work with a master teacher. This book has my highest recommendation."

-**Dennis Tirch, PhD,** author of 6 books,
Founding Director, The Center for Compassion Focused Therapy

"This is a treasure trove for clinicians who wish to integrate first, second and third wave cognitive-behavioral therapies in their work. Dr. Sears is a master clinician and meditation teacher who skillfully synthesized the essence of these approaches in succinct and scientifically grounded text. He also created a collection of handouts that are both engaging and simple to use. Both the handouts and the resources Dr. Sears has assembled will help clinicians and their clients effectively address many of the issues commonly brought to therapy."

-**Louanne Davis, PsyD,** author of *Meditations for Healing Trauma*,
clinical psychologist, certified MBSR instructor

Dedication

To my mother, my first and
best teacher of CBT and mindfulness

Table of Contents

John Ryongwan Paulson

Richard W. Sears, PsyD, PhD, MBA, ABPP, is a board-certified clinical psychologist in Cincinnati, Ohio, where he runs a private therapy and consultation practice, and is Director of the Center for Clinical Mindfulness & Meditation. He has practiced and taught mindfulness for over 30 years, and was full-time faculty for the PsyD Program at Union Institute & University for nine years. He is also clinical/research faculty at the University of Cincinnati Center for Integrative Health and Wellness and is Volunteer Associate Professor of Clinical Psychiatry & Behavioral Neurosciences with UC College of Medicine. Dr. Sears is a psychologist contractor with the Cincinnati VA Medical Center and with Alliance Integrative Medicine.

Dr. Sears is author of *Mindfulness in Clinical Practice* (with Dennis Tirch and Robert Denton), *Consultation Skills for Mental Health Professionals* (with John Rudisill and Carrie Mason-Sears), *Mindfulness: Living Through Challenges and Enriching Your Life*, *Building Competence in Mindfulness-Based Cognitive Therapy*, *MBCT for PTSD* (with Kathleen Chard), *The Sense of Self*, and *Hopes and Perspectives of Muslim American Women: A Paradox of Honor* (with Tayeba Shaikh and Jennifer Ossege). He is co-editor of the books *Perspectives on Spirituality and Religion in Psychotherapy* (with Alison Niblick) and *The Resilient Mental Health Practice* (with Jennifer Ossege).

He is also a fifth degree black belt in Ninjutsu, and once served briefly as a personal protection agent for the Dalai Lama. He has a PhD in Buddhist Studies, received ordination in three traditions, and received transmission as a Zen master from Wonji Dharma in the lineage of Seung Sahn.

You can also join an online group or listen to free recordings on Dr. Sears' website, www.psych-insights.com/mindfulness

Acknowledgements

This book is the culmination of years of teaching a workshop for mental health professionals on CBT and Mindfulness for PESI, Inc. I would like to begin by thanking the thousands of workshop participants who shared their ideas, passions, and questions, challenging me to continuously refine my own understanding. I would also like to thank the wonderful people at PESI and PESI Publishing & Media, including Emily Krumenauer, Claire Zelasko, Karsyn Morse, Hillary Jenness, Linda Jackson, and Shannon Becker. I especially appreciate Donald Altman's detailed editing and feedback on the manuscript.

I am also very appreciative of the support and inspiration of countless professional colleagues, friends, and mentors on the path of self-exploration, including the Dalai Lama, Wonji Dharma, Suhita Dharma, Steven C. Hayes, Stephen K. Hayes, Dennis Tirch, Zindel Segal, Jon Kabat-Zinn, Elana Rosenbaum, Susan Woods, Randye Semple, Jean Kristeller, Ryan Niemiec, Susan Albers, Sarah Bowen, Ruth Baer, Mark Lau, Alan Marlatt, Dan Siegel, Alan Watts, Sian Cotton, Melissa DelBello, Jeffery Strawn, Rachel Wasson, Kathleen Chard, Tina Luberto, Kristen Kraemer, Emily O'Bryan, Jennifer Ossege, Steve and Sandi Amoils, Robert Chong An Denton, Sharon Salzberg, David Kyutoshi Sink, David Piser, John Ryongwan Paulson, Sunyananda Dharma, Hwasahn Prajna, and James Myo Gak Foster, to name but a few.

I am especially thankful for the love and support of my family, and for their patience with my countless days of traveling to give workshops: Carrie Mason-Sears, Ashlyn Sears, Caylee Sears, Jeremy Rogers, Olivia and Brittney Taylor, Charles and Elfriede Sears, Linda and John Coghill, and Brad, Nick, and Camryn Mason.

Finally, I would like to thank my students and clients for sharing so much of their suffering and their joys with me. I feel honored and privileged to have shared such profound human journeys with them.

Introduction

I have been traveling for years giving workshops for PESI called "Cognitive Behavioral Therapy and Mindfulness: An Integrative, Evidence-Based Approach." Many people are surprised to see such a combination of seemingly opposite approaches. In their minds, cognitive behavioral therapy (CBT) is based on solid, scientifically researched principles, while they may have a misconception that mindfulness is some kind of "touchy-freely" approach.

People often tell me that they attend my CBT and Mindfulness workshops because their agency will pay for a CBT workshop, but might not pay for a mindfulness workshop. However, the mindfulness-based interventions I will be discussing in this book, such as Mindfulness-Based Cognitive Therapy (MBCT: Segal, Williams, & Teasdale, 2013), Acceptance and Commitment Therapy (ACT: Hayes, Strosahl, & Wilson, 2012), and Dialectical Behavior Therapy (DBT: Linehan, 2015a, 2015b) are all considered evidence-based practices (APA Division 12, 2016). In fact, their evidence ratings are at least a strong as CBT. In the clinical research literature, mindfulness-based approaches build nicely upon the solid research foundation laid by studies of CBT principles. There is also a rapidly growing amount of brain imaging research supporting the effectiveness of mindfulness practice (Tang, Hölzel, & Posner, 2015).

One of the problems is that many people use the word "mindfulness" very loosely. Sometimes I meet clinicians who say, "I do mindfulness in my clinical work."

"Wonderful," I'll reply. "In what ways do you use it?"

"I sit with the client in silence for about five minutes at the beginning of the session."

"Okay," I respond encouragingly. "Then what?"

"Well," they say with a slightly confused tone, "then we just do therapy for the rest of the hour."

While being silent might be a wonderful way for clients to settle down and prepare their minds before the therapy session, sitting in silence does not necessarily mean one is being mindful, and it is definitely not the same as using evidence-based, structured approaches like MBCT, ACT, and DBT.

Another source of confusion is that people often use the word mindfulness interchangeably with the word meditation. However, meditation is actually a broad term that refers to many different methods for working with the mind. Mindfulness is a very specific type of meditation, which basically involves consciously placing one's attention in the present moment.

MY OWN PATH TO MINDFULNESS

As you use this book, you will be developing your own path to mindfulness. My interest in teaching CBT and mindfulness probably goes back to when I was a teenager and I wanted to become a ninja. Far from what is depicted in the turtle movies, the ninja arts emphasize self-development, becoming an actualized human being. The ninja are known as "the invisible warriors." The real meaning of this is that we practice setting up our lives in such a way that we do not attract the attention of anyone who would seek to harm us. Though ninjutsu is known as a martial art, in a broader sense it is a system of strategy and development. We try not to make targets of ourselves, and work to prevent conflict from ever arising. When important things need to be done in the world, we work to subtly set

up the causes and conditions to make them happen, instead of making a big show of it. Marici, an Asian symbol of the ultimate warrior, holds a leaf in one hand to cover the eyes of potential enemies, and a needle and thread to sew the eyelids shut of those who would do harm in the world.

I became fascinated by the books of Stephen K. Hayes, the first Westerner to live in Japan and study with the last living ninja grandmaster, Masaaki Hatsumi (Hayes, 2013). Mr. Hayes lives not far from me, in Dayton, Ohio, and has been my mentor and friend for over 30 years.

During my ninja training, I quickly learned that to develop my potential, and to make the world a better place, I needed to develop my mind, which is what drew me to the meditative traditions. While I had mentors who were very practical, I also had teachers who were very traditional in their training approach. Some of them emphasized the "just sit there for 20 years and it will all come to you" method. While such training has its merits, I found myself ill-equipped to deal with the modern, real-world problems that my students were bringing to me. This is what eventually led me to enter a doctoral program in clinical psychology. I was fortunate to receive very broad clinical training that included a strong emphasis on issues of diversity and cultural competence, and I was able to do almost everything psychologists are allowed to do in their scope of practice.

I got involved in some exciting new research, including using mindfulness-based cognitive therapy for veterans with posttraumatic stress disorder (Sears & Chard, 2016), fMRI brain scan research on kids with anxiety and mood disorders (Cotton, Luberto, Sears, Strawn, Wasson, & DelBello, 2015; Strawn, Cotton, Luberto, Patino, Stahl, et al., 2016), and using a brief MBCT intervention in hospital settings for clinicians and administrators (Luberto, Wasson, Kraemer, Sears, Hueber, & Cotton, 2017). My passion is to de-mystify the research and practices and help as many clients and other clinicians as possible. **To that end, the integrative mindfulness and cognitive-behavioral therapy handouts, worksheets, and tips contained in this book offer you specific tools and techniques that you can immediately incorporate into your clinical work with clients.**

A QUICK PRIMER FOR UNDERSTANDING CBT AND MINDFULNESS

The development and evolution of first behavioral, then cognitive, and finally mindfulness therapies is a fascinating one. Each is an important extension of the one that preceded it, and that's why these therapies fit well when used together. While my workshops and other sources can help anyone establish a deeper foundation in the principles of behavioral therapy, cognitive therapy, and how mindfulness is used in a clinical context, for the purposes of this book we'll stick to how they are applied in the handouts. (If you're already very familiar with each of these therapies, feel free to skip ahead.)

The three basic therapies in this book help people change because they have been shown to shift how one behaves, thinks, and experiences what is happening in each moment. What is more, these changes are mirrored in a subtle rewiring of the brain. **Behavior therapy is known as the "first wave" of CBT,** and the most important concepts for our clinical work involve classical and operant conditioning.

Classical conditioning is much like building a roadway in the brain. The first time you build a road, it takes a lot of time to dig up the ground, lay the foundation, and top it with asphalt. If you stop using that roadway, it is likely to start falling apart, and weeds will start growing in the cracks. However, the next time you want to start using that roadway, you will be able to get it operational much more quickly.

This concept is also very important in applying the tools in this book. Perhaps you can recall a client who came to you with a problem like anxiety, and after you did the great clinical work that you always do, they got better, and they went away. Yet, a couple of months later, or a couple of years later, they came back to your office with the exact same issue they presented with the first time. One of the reasons this happens is that they are falling back into those old conditioned brain pathways, into those maladaptive "brain grooves" so to speak. That's why you'll want to help clients apply the skills on a consistent basis. This is especially true when working with mood disorders because the more often clients get depressed, the more likely they are to get depressed again.

Then there's operant conditioning, which is also an integral part of this book. Positive reinforcement is what people think of most often in relation to operant conditioning. If I do something, and get something I want as a result, I am more likely to keep doing that behavior. The reinforcer could be something tangible, like food, or something intangible, like social praise.

When I was a graduate student, Temple Grandin, a speaker who has a doctorate degree, and who also has autism, came to do a grand rounds at the hospital where I was working. She gave a wonderful, engaging presentation, and had a delightful sense of humor. After the presentation a number of students approached her to ask questions, and I carefully listened in.

Someone asked her, "You said that with your autism, you have trouble with social situations, and you don't really understand most people's humor very well. But your presentation was amazing, and your jokes were hilarious. How do you do it?"

"It's easy," Dr. Grandin quickly replied. "Whenever I say something that makes everybody laugh, I just remember to say it again the next time I speak." That's positive reinforcement. Positive reinforcement becomes especially important when working with small children and their caregivers. Even helping your clients notice small, positive changes can be self-reinforcing. This theme will be revisited throughout various handouts.

Now, there's a lot more to understanding what makes behavioral therapy effective, such as negative reinforcement, which is a major factor in addiction. When people experience unpleasant feelings like cravings or anxiety, they naturally do not want to feel it. When they take a drink of alcohol, the feeling immediately goes down a little, negatively reinforcing whatever they just did. Basically, the brain says, "Whatever you just did, I don't feel as bad as I did a moment ago, so do more of that." Of course, the effect of the alcohol is only temporary, and the cravings and emotions come back again.

Several interventions in this book address how people often go to great lengths in their attempts to avoid feeling unpleasant emotions or body sensations. Because what they do works in the short term, they get caught in a negative reinforcement loop, and have a hard time stopping the avoidance behaviors. That's why a conscious understanding of behavioral reinforcement is crucial.

Cognitive therapy is considered the "second wave" of CBT, which came along as a reaction to the radical behaviorist view that we are simply mindless animals. This therapy acknowledges that our thinking has a significant impact on our behavior. In fact, thoughts themselves can be considered behaviors that can be conditioned or reinforced (Torneke, Barnes-Holmes, & Hayes, 2010). Cognitive therapy can be succinctly summarized with the "ABC" model. A stands for "antecedent," or "activating event." B could stand for behavior in a behavioral model, but in cognitive therapy, it stands for "beliefs," or the thoughts about what is happening. C is for "consequence," or what happens next, which could be an emotion or a behavior (Burns, 1989; Ellis & Grieger, 1977; Trower, Casey, & Dryden, 1998).

While it is common sense to therapists, it is often a major paradigm shift for clients to recognize that their thoughts affect the way they feel, and that their feelings affect their thinking.

I was once driving to a hospital to lead a group on mindfulness and stress reduction. Someone ahead of me pulled into the left turn lane, somewhat erratically. As I was moving forward in the lane with a straight ahead arrow, the car suddenly jerked back right in front of me, barely missing my car. My immediate thoughts were about how rude and inconsiderate the driver was, which led to a feeling of irritation. However, just a short time later, I watched the person pull directly up to the emergency room entrance. I quickly realized that they must have had a life-threatening emergency, and politeness was of course a lower priority for them. My feelings immediately changed to empathy and compassion, with a tinge of embarrassment.

Sometimes clients have trouble recognizing the beliefs and thoughts they are having. In Part 2, Cognitive Tools, an upcoming handout explores "automatic thoughts," those thoughts that seemingly pop up out of nowhere, which we may barely notice. Yet such thoughts can have a profound impact on our emotions and behaviors. It can take practice to develop more awareness of our own thoughts, especially in challenging situations. The good news is that by pausing to explore the B, we can interrupt the seemingly automatic pattern of jumping from A to C. This pausing to notice thoughts, and making a conscious choice rather than an automatic reaction, can help prevent a lot of unnecessary problems.

Traditional CBT emphasizes disputing, challenging or weighing the evidence for or against a maladaptive or irrational thought. The idea is that by changing the thought, the person will experience a different emotion. While CBT works very well for many clients, have you ever had this happen? Let's say a client identifies a maladaptive thought, such as, "I can't do anything right."

You might challenge that thought, perhaps saying, "How true do you think that thought is? What is the evidence that you can't do *anything* right?"

"Well," they quickly respond, "I got kicked out of school, I got fired from three jobs, and I got divorced."

"But your partner was just as responsible as you were for that relationship not working out," you offer.

"Yeah, but I'm the idiot that picked that partner in the first place!"

Because of the principle of mood state-dependent memory, the cards are stacked against clients who are struggling, especially when they are trying to dispute their own thoughts. If the client is already depressed, they can quickly and easily come up with depressing thoughts, and it is hard for them to find more rational counter-thoughts.

CBT is an empirically supported treatment, and it obviously works. Surprisingly, however, it turns out that if you do CBT without the challenging or disputation component, it still works just as well (Longmore & Worrell, 2007; Sears, Tirch, & Denton, 2011). "Wait a minute!" you might be thinking. "I thought that challenging thoughts was the heart of CBT!" Well, according to the research, if you do not challenge a client's thoughts, CBT still works just as well. What's going on here?

That leads us to mindfulness-based therapies, and a process known as "decentering" (Piaget, 1950; Piaget & Morf, 1958; Segal, Williams, & Teasdale, 2013), which Acceptance and Commitment Therapy calls "defusion" (Hayes, Strosahl, & Wilson, 2012). Normally, clients become over-identified with their thoughts, as if they are in the center of them, or as if they are "fused" to them. It may sound like semantics, but instead of getting caught up in a thought like, "I'm a terrible person," clients can learn to recognize, "I am *having a thought* that I'm a terrible person." Effectively, clients learn to uncouple their thoughts, which are simply internalized words, from their conditioned meanings and emotional associations.

Mindfulness has become known as the "third wave" of cognitive behavioral therapies (Fletcher & Hayes, 2005; Hayes, 2004; Segal, Teasdale, & Williams, 2004). Years ago, when I was teaching a doctoral course on CBT, the authors of our textbook basically stated that it remained to be seen if mindfulness would actually be the third wave of CBT, or if it was only a passing fad. When I attended an Association for Behavioral and Cognitive Therapy (ABCT) conference a few years ago, it seemed like nearly half of all presentations involved mindfulness, so it is clearly now in the mainstream. A number of mindfulness-based interventions now have strong evidence-based practice ratings. There are countless books, associations, research articles, and even journals dedicated to the study of interventions utilizing mindfulness. The publication *Mindfulness Research Monthly* lists dozens and dozens of new studies coming out every single month. Since mindfulness simply means paying attention, I certainly hope that it continues to remain in vogue.

Though mindfulness has always been a natural capacity of being human, and has been taught by various traditions for thousands of years, systematic research has only been rigorously done in recent decades. One of the primary pioneers in the clinical applications of mindfulness is Jon Kabat-Zinn, along with his colleagues at the University of Massachusetts Medical Center, who began developing and researching an eight-week program known as Mindfulness-Based Stress Reduction (MBSR: Kabat-Zinn, 2013).

Even though the word mindfulness is growing increasingly popular, the term is often misused and misunderstood. For our clinical work, it is important to be clear about what mindfulness is, and how it differs from other types of meditation or interventions. Jon Kabat-Zinn defines mindfulness as, "The awareness that emerges, through paying attention, in a particular way, on purpose, in the present moment, nonjudgmentally, to the unfolding of experience from moment to moment" (Kabat-Zinn, 1994, p. 4; Kabat-Zinn, 2003, p. 145). Each of these terms will be highlighted in the various mindfulness-oriented handouts you'll be using.

One important point for you as the reader is that I will be emphasizing the clinical utility of mindfulness throughout these pages, but I do not wish to take away from the many other applications of mindfulness, such as for spiritual growth. I also do not intend to imply that the principles and techniques described here are the best or only way to utilize cognitive behavioral therapy, or that everyone needs to practice mindfulness in a specific way.

Sometimes therapists tell me that they want to learn ways to more effectively "sell" mindfulness to their clients, but I never "sell" mindfulness to anyone. I am a clinician first, and use whatever tools will most likely be helpful to my clients. Of course, it is hard to imagine that paying attention will not be helpful for someone who is suffering, and there are many ways to develop one's attentional capacity.

Most importantly, practice the mindfulness exercises yourself. Question the material and look up other sources of information and research. Consider how these principles might apply to your own clinical work. Ponder how both you and your clients might benefit from what you are learning. Ideally, join a mindfulness training program near you. You can also join an online group or listen to free recordings on my website.

Hopefully, the material about mindfulness will make intuitive sense to you, and I highly encourage you to develop your own personal mindfulness practice. Only then will you make these skills and attitudes consistently and reliably your own.

HOW TO USE THIS BOOK

I recommend that you begin by familiarizing yourself with the material and exercises in Parts 1, 2, and 3, since these cover fundamental concepts that apply to all of the CBT and mindfulness interventions in these pages. This may be a good starting point for clients, too, because they will start to understand the power of thoughts and how thoughts and behavior are linked. For ease of use, the Table of Contents lists all the handouts and worksheets so that you can reference them quickly, since handouts and/or worksheets in one section might easily apply to other presenting issues. For example, the worksheet entitled, "When Strong Thoughts Just Won't Go Away" is in Part 4 in the OCD section, but the worksheet may be useful for a wide variety of presenting issues.

If you find my mindfulness recordings useful, you are welcome to share them with clients. You are also welcome to photocopy the handouts and worksheets in this book to give to clients. Even though you are likely already giving clients good information, it can be helpful for them to hear it in multiple ways, and it can be useful for them to work on material between sessions.

I should mention from the beginning that it is entirely possible that I will offend almost everyone who reads this book at some point. I like to use humor to add a light touch to this often very serious content, and I also like to over-exaggerate my points sometimes, and these things may not come across well in the written word. I apologize in advance for this, though my guess is that as a mental health professional, being offended will not be a new experience for you.

Part 1

Behavioral Tools

Before diving into the behavioral analysis worksheet here, it's worth noting just how many different schools of psychotherapy there are. Prochaska and Norcross (2010) have noted that there are at least 880 different, distinct schools of psychotherapy. How can there be so many different ways of doing therapy, all claiming to be the "right" way? The research even supports that most of these therapies work, which has been called the "Dodo Bird effect," from Alice in Wonderland, "All have won, and all must have prizes" (Rosenzweig, 1936).

Researchers have done meta-analyses to discover the common factors underlying all these seemingly different approaches (Duncan, Miller, Wampold, & Hubble, 2010). Though the numbers vary depending on how the meta-analyses are done, the research done by Bruce Wampold is commonly cited (Wampold & Imel, 2015). It appears that 40% of change in psychotherapy is due to extratherapeutic factors. Clients bring their own innate strengths to the psychotherapy process, such as perseverance or risk-taking. Or something happens in their environment that sparks a change — they get a new job, they join a spiritual community, or their partner gets more involved. In other words, the biggest percentage of change is happening outside the therapy room. Of course, knowing this, we can work with clients to improve their relationships and connect them to resources.

The next biggest change factor is the therapeutic relationship, which accounts for 30% of the variance. We all know that having good rapport and a strong working alliance is essential for all of psychotherapy. Because the therapeutic relationship matters, be careful not to make positive reinforcement too forced or artificial. I once had a radical behaviorist supervisor who, on several occasions after a supervision session, suddenly remembered that he had not given me any positive reinforcement. He would fumblingly call out something like, "Um, good job getting that report in to me on time." It felt so insincere that it probably would have been better for him to say nothing. On the other hand, sincerely letting family, friends, and coworkers know how much you appreciate them will often make their entire day.

TIPS ABOUT SCHEDULES OF REINFORCEMENT

Schedules of reinforcement, which involve the consistency and reliability of reinforcement, are very important factors in changing behavior (Domjan 2008; Ferster & Skinner, 1957; Schoenfeld, 1970). As in the examples above, if you want to start any new behavior, it is important to reward that behavior very consistently, very predictably, and very reliably. You are more likely to make a change if you know for sure that it will pay off. It is very heart-breaking when young children make efforts to change, but their caregivers do not notice or reinforce the positive changes they are making.

The hardest behaviors to get rid of are those that have been intermittently reinforced. Gambling is a classic example of this principle. When people pull the lever of a slot machine, there is a chance they could win thousands of dollars. Individuals who succumb to the gambler's fallacy are prone to think, "I've already lost a thousand times in a row, surely the next pull of this lever will be a winner!" (Ayton & Fischer, 2004). While it is true that we can use statistics to determine that someone should win once in every one thousand tries, the fact is, in each moment, the odds are exactly the same. In the moment after losing one thousand times, the odds are still the same as they were the very first time the person pulled the lever — one in a thousand. However, because there is chance that they might win, and because they also feel so much guilt and shame about all the money they have already lost, it can be difficult to stop pulling that lever.

APPLYING BEHAVIORAL PRINCIPLES: THE CASE OF THE FLYING PACIFIER

Before using the behavioral analysis worksheet, the "Case of the Flying Pacifier" is a good example of how to deconstruct behavior. I once worked with a couple with a young baby who was waking up all night. The sleep-deprived couple were at their wit's end trying to figure out what to do. When I asked them what was going on, they said the baby kept throwing her pacifier out of the crib and onto the floor, then crying loudly. When I asked how they responded, they said they immediately ran up to the room, picked up the pacifier, gave it back to the baby, then picked her up and cuddled with her. The baby would be fine for a while, but then a little later, would throw the pacifier again, and start crying again. This could happen a dozen or more times every night.

I explained to them that it appeared as though their brilliant child had learned how to immediately get hugs and kisses from mommy and daddy. Since she could sleep whenever she wanted, she did not care what time of night it was. Because the parents were always giving the pacifier back, along with lots of cuddling, they were reinforcing the throwing and crying.

According to behavioral principles, the parents basically had two options for breaking this behavior. They could choose to simply not pick up the pacifier, and not to respond to the baby's crying. However, this is really hard to do, as it is heart-wrenching and seems very inhumane to let your child cry for hours.

My suggestion was to save the attention and cuddling for daylight hours. When the baby cried, the parents should simply pick up the pacifier, give it back to the baby, and leave the room. Since the baby would really want the cuddles, I warned them about the "extinction burst" that was likely to happen at first. She would likely throw the pacifier a lot more to get the attention she wanted.

Sure enough, the baby threw the pacifier out of the crib about 80 times the first night the parents tried this. To their credit, the parents were able to stick with just picking it up, giving it back to the baby, and not reinforcing her with hugs and kisses. The next night, it only happened 50 times. The following night, 20 times. The night after that, 10 times. After that night, the baby stopped throwing her pacifier, and the exhausted parents were once again able to sleep through the night.

While the principles of classical and operant conditioning are very simple, they can be applied in many ways to a variety of seemingly intractable problems. Pay attention to what may be reinforcing the behavior. Consider what got the problem behavior started, and what might be keeping it going, as well as how to extinguish it. This worksheet will help, and can be used by you or by your clients.

Analyzing Behavior

Some behaviors can appear very baffling to us at first, seeming random and impossible to control. However, through careful observation, we are likely to discover that there are underlying causes and conditions for the behaviors. Use this worksheet to help you investigate and understand problem behaviors.

In as much detail as you can, write out exactly what the problem behavior is.

_____

_____

_____

_____

_____

_____

_____

How often does the behavior occur? How intense does it get? How long does it last?

_____

_____

_____

_____

_____

_____

_____

Behaviors do not occur in a vacuum. In what context(s) does this behavior occur? Consider a wide variety of environmental factors like setting, people, and time of day.

_____

_____

_____

_____

_____

_____

_____

How do other people react to the problem behavior? What do other people do during and after the problem behavior?

_____

_____

_____

_____

_____

_____

Consider what classical conditioning may have taken place. Are there specific stimuli or triggers associated with this behavior, either now or in the past? What is going on right before the problem behavior?

_____

_____

_____

_____

_____

_____

Behaviors often continue because the person is getting something from them. What are the positive reinforcers? What might be gained from this behavior, either now or in the past? (attention, an object, a pleasant activity, etc.)

_____

_____

_____

_____

_____

Some behaviors continue due to negative reinforcement. What might this behavior help the person avoid? (an unpleasant activity, a person they don't like, a strong emotion, etc.)

_____

_____

_____

_____

_____

_____

What are some alternative ways the person might achieve their desired goals?

_____

_____

_____

_____

_____

Sometimes, directly fighting an old behavior only makes it a bigger issue. It can often be more helpful to reinforce or reward a new, more appropriate behavior. What are some alternative behaviors that you can differentially reinforce? (For example, if you praise a child for creatively playing with clay, they are less likely to use their hands for hitting siblings.)

_____

_____

_____

_____

_____

Don't forget to pay attention to the positive qualities of the person. What are the person's strengths? Is there a context in which the "problem" behavior might be/have been appropriate? How can the person's strengths be helpful in moving toward change?

_____

_____

_____

_____

_____

_____

༺⚬༻

Remember to be patient as you investigate this problem behavior, as it may have become a deeply ingrained, nearly unconscious habit. Work to avoid inadvertently reinforcing the old behaviors, and be quick to reinforce even small changes in the direction of improvement. Experiment with interventions, knowing that the behavior may get a little worse at first, and let the outcome determine if what you are doing is really working. If your initial intervention fails, and the behavior continues, go back through the entire worksheet again until you discover what you were missing.

Part 2

Cognitive Tools

Addressing maladaptive thoughts is an important part of cognitive therapy. Sometimes the clinician needs to help the client dig below the surface to discover core beliefs, or deeply held patterns of thinking. At an even deeper level, schemas are the ways our brains interpret patterns of information to make sense of the world. Amusingly, when my youngest daughter was in first grade, one of her first homework assignments was about schemas. I told her that most adults do not even know what a schema is. Her homework sheet had questions like, "What is your schema for an apple?" She wrote down things like, "they are red, crunchy, and delicious."

Two people can be experiencing the exact same event at the exact same time, yet have two completely different interpretations of what they are witnessing. You might be enjoying a gorgeous sunset full of beautiful colors, but the person next to you might be a Debbie Downer type, who says, "Actually, all those beautiful colors are due to pollution in the atmosphere."

Individuals who suffer from disorders like posttraumatic stress disorder and major depressive disorder are especially likely to have negatively biased schemas, as will be explored in future handouts and worksheets.

TIPS FOR WORKING WITH EMOTIONAL STATES

Just as our thoughts affect our emotional states, our emotional states can affect our thinking. An important concept to remember when working with thoughts and emotions is known as "mood state-dependent memory" (Ucros, 1989). Basically, when you learn something when you are in a certain mood or emotional state, you are more likely to remember it the next time you are in that state. When I taught this concept in undergraduate classes, I once had a student ask, "Does this mean that if I'm drunk when I'm studying, I should be drunk when I take the exam?" My response was, "Well, that's the principle, but that's a bad idea in practice."

In clinical practice, what this means is that if clients are in a depressed mood, their brains will have fast and easy access to memories of other times in the past when they felt depressed. It will be easy to remember and think about unpleasant things, and difficult for them to bring to mind positive things.

The opposite is also true. Do you have one of those "annoyingly happy" friends? When they are feeling happy, they frequently talk about all the great things going on, and it takes some effort or bad circumstances to get them to think more about unpleasant things.

The handouts and worksheets that follow will help clients understand and practice the important principles of cognitive therapy. Note that most of these handouts involve recognition of troublesome thinking, rather than telling clients what to do about them. Recognition is an important first step. Remember, too, that compulsively trying to change thoughts often gives them more power—which is why the "decentering" process mentioned earlier can be useful. Suggestions for specific interventions will be given in later sections and handouts/worksheets.

Gratitude List

Years ago, I had an interesting experience in a meditation class run by one of my mentors, Stephen K. Hayes. The class was held in the evening, so I had already had a long, intense day of working. It was also an hour away, so I had to fight rush hour traffic to get to the class. I made it literally at the last second, just as someone was locking the door so the class could begin meditating without interruption.

As soon as I sat down, Mr. Hayes began leading us through a meditation on gratitude. He asked us to reflect back over the day on all of the positive or pleasant events we had experienced. Since I had just been frantically dodging traffic, I could not come up with a single positive thing at first. However, as my mind began to settle, a memory suddenly popped up that I had enjoyed the taste of a cup of coffee that morning. I then remembered that breakfast had been rather tasty. I then remembered that my very young daughter had told me a cute joke that made me laugh out loud. Before long, my mind was flooded with countless small moments of pleasantness. When I was feeling stressed, they were not readily available to my mind, and I may not have even been very aware of just how pleasant those things were as I was experiencing them.

When you are in a particular mood, thoughts and memories related to that mood are more easy to access. When you are feeling stressed, the brain is more likely to bring to mind things that are stressful. **By consciously paying attention to the good things in our lives, we can overcome the automatic tendency to look for the negative.** Research has shown that even writing down a few things that you are grateful for even once a week can increase your happiness.

In the space below, write down the people, things, and experiences that you are grateful for. Ideally, find a quiet, peaceful place to sit and allow your mind to open up a little. It may feel a little forced at first, but watch to see what comes up for you. Look back over this list from time to time to renew your appreciation. If you repeat this exercise once a week, you might even notice the pleasant side effect of your happiness increasing a little.

People I am grateful for:

_____

_____

_____

_____

_____

Things I am grateful for:

_____

_____

_____

_____

_____

Experiences and memories I am grateful for:

_____

_____

_____

_____

_____

I am also grateful for:

_____

_____

_____

_____

_____

Thought Records

It takes practice to become aware of the fact that our thoughts affect the way we feel, and that our feelings affect the kinds of thoughts we are likely to have. At the end of the day, reflect back on any distressing events you experienced, and use this worksheet to practice noticing the thoughts and feelings that came up for you, and how they might have affected each other. This will help you better understand what happened, so that you will feel less helpless when distressing situations, thoughts, and feelings come up in the future.

What happened? What was the situation?

_____

_____

_____

What were you feeling at the time?

_____

_____

_____

What were you thinking at the time?

_____

_____

_____

What other ways could you think about the event? If each of those alternative thoughts were true, how would you feel? (Try to list a number of different thoughts you *could* have had, and how each of those thoughts would likely have made you feel.)

_____

_____

_____

What can you do proactively to check out the truth of the situation, to see if your thoughts are accurate? What can you do to deal with the situation, or other future situations like that, more constructively?

_____

_____

_____

Recognizing Automatic Thoughts

All of us experience thoughts that happen so quickly and automatically that we are barely even aware of them. Sometimes these automatic thoughts are very useful. I often wear a wireless microphone when I'm giving presentations, and whenever I go to the bathroom during a break, I automatically think of the actor Leslie Nielson. In the movie *Police Squad*, he forgets to turn off his wireless microphone, and the entire audience hears a loud broadcast of his bodily functions in the restroom. This automatic thought reminds me to make sure I turned off my microphone, and I'm sure my audiences appreciate that.

In some circumstances, automatic thoughts create trouble for us. When we are completely unaware of them, they have a way of becoming a kind of self-fulfilling prophecy. I once worked with a lonely woman who automatically thought that no one would ever find her interesting or attractive. That thought made her put up an emotional wall, and she therefore came across as cold and disinterested. This prevented people from getting close to her, perpetuating her loneliness.

It is certainly normal to have automatic thoughts, and some of them may even be accurate once in a while. However, when they keep coming constantly, and when we get sucked into always believing them, it is a sign that we are stressed out, anxious, depressed, or overwhelmed.

Fighting distressing thoughts with more thoughts often just leads to a vicious cycle of struggle. The key is to notice them without getting caught up in their drama. The more you practice becoming aware of them as they arise, the less power they have over you.

Stepping back and watching your distressing thoughts can be like watching a scary horror movie. The first time you see a good, chilling movie, you are lost in the action, sitting on the edge of your seat, and jumping every time something frightening happens. However, after you have seen the same movie 100 times, nothing surprises you. It is easy to remember that it is just a movie, and it unfolds in the same way every single time it plays. You know what is coming, and you know that in reality, you are only watching flickering lights projected on a screen.

The thoughts in your head are no more than electrical impulses in your brain. While you may have some very real things to deal with in your life, thoughts themselves have no power other than what we give them. The most important thing is to recognize automatic thoughts and check them out before you act on them.

Take a look at the list on the next page, and see if any of these thoughts ever come up for you. There are also some blank spaces for you to write down other thoughts. Try to identify your own "top 10 hit parade" of thoughts that come up when you are getting overwhelmed. On a scale of 1-5, rate how often you have these thoughts, and how much you actually believe them or buy into them.

If you have a number of these thoughts very often, and you believe them, it will be important to seek professional help right away. As your mood improves, you will be able to monitor these thoughts as a sign of how you are doing. It will be a good sign when you do not really believe the thoughts even if they are coming up frequently.

Recognizing Automatic Thoughts

On a scale of 1-5, rate how often you have these thoughts, and how much you actually believe them or buy into them.

	How often? (1=never, 5=very often)	How much do you believe it? (1=not at all, 5=absolutely true)
Nothing will ever get better.		
I can't stand this anymore.		
I'm not good enough.		
There is something wrong with me.		
I'm such a loser.		
The world is a terrible place.		
I wish I was never born.		
Why bother with anything.		
It's just not worth it.		
Everyone else is better off than me.		
Why does everything always happen to me?		
I just can't do anything right.		
I hate myself.		
People are such jerks.		
No one cares about me.		
I'll never be loved.		
I'm unlovable.		
I just can't do this anymore.		
Life sucks.		
Things will never get better.		
I'll never stop feeling this way.		
My life is over.		
I'm a bad person for all the awful things I've done in the past.		

Recognizing
Troublesome Thinking Patterns

Thinking is a very important and powerful tool, but it is far from perfect. Sometimes certain old patterns can intrude into the present and hijack our thinking, distorting our perceptions of reality. Even blatantly untrue thoughts can sometimes seem very convincing when we get lost in them.

Look through the list of troublesome thinking patterns below. Do you ever get hooked by any of these? The first step in working with them is to notice them for what they are. It is often easy to see other people engaging in these patterns, or even to laugh at how absurd they sound when you read them, but they can be hard to notice when you are caught up in them. Take a few minutes to consider each one of these patterns to see if you can recognize how they might show up in your own thinking at times. If any of these apply to you, make notes to yourself so you can get better at seeing the signs of when they hook your mind.

It is important not to judge yourself too harshly when you do notice you are thinking in one of these ways. It may very well be that you did experience a catastrophe in the past, or someone really did think what you thought they were thinking. The most important thing is to notice your thinking patterns and to see how well they fit your current situation. Remember, too, that everyone at some point in their lives experiences these different styles of thinking.

CATASTROPHIZING

In this pattern of troublesome thinking, you get a small piece of bad news, and your mind carries you off to all kinds of other possible, though highly unlikely, scenarios that are much worse.

> **Example:** "My friend is late. Maybe he was in a car accident. He could be hurt really badly. What if he never walks again? He has to walk at his job, so he won't be able to work anymore. He has two kids — how will he feed his family if he can't work? What if he can't pay his mortgage and they all become homeless?"

Can you think of an example of when you have done this in the past?

_____

_____

_____

Are there any areas of your life where you are doing this now?

_____

_____

_____

What are the situations in which you are most likely to think this way?

_____

_____

_____

_____

GENERALIZING

This pattern involves noticing one specific thing, situation, or quality, and automatically believing that it applies much more broadly. Nothing goes well all the time, but it doesn't mean everything will go badly all the time.

> **Example:** "When I tried to fix the garage door, I completely messed it up. I just can't do anything right."

Can you think of an example of when you have done this in the past?

_____

_____

_____

_____

Are there any areas of your life where you are doing this now?

_____

_____

_____

_____

What are the situations in which you are most likely to think this way?

_____

_____

_____

_____

BLACK AND WHITE THINKING

Our brains often want to categorize things as this or that, good or bad, all or nothing, black or white. However, in reality, there are many shades of gray. There are variations in good and bad in every person, thing, and situation, and these can also change with time. Someone can be a nice person but still be somewhat selfish. Someone can be direct in ways that often come across as rude but still be a fairly decent person.

Example: "He called me to ask how I was doing when no one else did, so I thought he was the greatest guy on Earth. Now he's an hour late and hasn't bothered calling – turns out he's the biggest jerk on Earth."

Can you think of an example of when you have done this in the past?

_____

_____

_____

_____

Are there any areas of your life where you are doing this now?

_____

_____

_____

_____

What are the situations in which you are most likely to think this way?

_____

_____

_____

_____

FOCUSING ON WEAKNESSES AND FORGETTING STRENGTHS

Our brains have evolved to pay more attention to the negative. While this helps us survive threats, in modern society, it makes for a very pessimistic outlook on life. Nobody can be good at everything – we all have strengths as well as weaknesses. When you find yourself focusing on the faults of yourself or others, or seeing the worst in every situation, remind yourself that there are things you can do well, and that other people have at least a few good qualities.

Example: Forgetting all the hard work you did to raise a family and the skills it took you to survive countless crises, you think, "I'm such a loser for not being better at using computers."

Can you think of an example of when you have done this in the past?

_____

_____

_____

_____

Are there any areas of your life where you are doing this now?

_____

_____

_____

_____

What are the situations in which you are most likely to think this way?

_____

_____

_____

_____

MIND READING

Sometimes we think we know what another person is thinking, and then get upset that they are thinking that. In reality, we can never truly know what another person is thinking, and continuously trying to guess tends to get us worked up.

> **Example:** "I worked really hard on my appearance today, and my boyfriend didn't say a word about it. I bet he thinks I'm ugly. He probably expects me to look like a TV model. What a shallow man! Who is he to judge me?! I don't need that jerk in my life!"

Can you think of an example of when you have done this in the past?

_____

_____

_____

_____

Are there any areas of your life where you are doing this now?

_____

_____

_____

_____

What are the situations in which you are most likely to think this way?

_____

_____

_____

CRYSTAL BALL GAZING

This pattern of thinking involves getting caught up in endless "what if" scenarios in our minds, and getting upset by them. The truth is, we can never know the future with complete certainty, and even though bad things do happen, not every single bad thing we can think of will actually happen.

Example: "I really don't want to give that speech at work tomorrow. Everyone is going to hate my ideas. They will attack me until I cry. I'll probably get fired, and no other company will ever want to hire someone who got fired, so I'll live out the rest of my life in poverty."

Can you think of an example of when you have done this in the past?

_____

_____

_____

_____

Are there any areas of your life where you are doing this now?

_____

_____

_____

_____

What are the situations in which you are most likely to think this way?

_____

_____

_____

_____

PUTTING YOURSELF OR OTHERS IN A "NO-WIN" SITUATION

In our minds, we sometimes put ourselves or others into a "darned if you do, darned if you don't" scenario. We somehow believe that whatever we or someone else does, it's wrong. At the root of this, we feel a deep sense of frustration or anxiety, and since that feeling is not going away, we are dissatisfied with every choice.

Self example: "There's no way I'm buying those big pants, I'm not that overweight. These blasted pants are too tight!"

Other example: When your child asks, "What's for dinner," you think, "Why doesn't that lazy child just check for herself?" However, if she does go up to check the food, you think, "Why is she messing with my cooking?"

Can you think of an example of when you have done this in the past?

_____

_____

_____

_____

Are there any areas of your life where you are doing this now?

_____

_____

_____

_____

What are the situations in which you are most likely to think this way?

_____

_____

_____

_____

"SHOULDING" AND "MUSTERBATION"

The late Albert Ellis was quite a character. He would tell clients, "Stop shoulding all over yourself," and talk about the problems with "musterbation" (Ellis & Harper, 1975). Words such as "should" and "must" cause endless problems in human thinking. Alan Watts (2004) once told an apocryphal story that God was writing a dictionary of all the words that would be used in human language. However, when visiting the archangel Gabriel, he had left the dictionary in the taxi. The devil got into the taxi, found the dictionary, and inserted the words "ought" and "should."

Many of us have deep down beliefs about how the world should work and what we must do. However, life is often not fair, and there is nothing we can do to change the past. All humans make mistakes, so the best we can do is work to repair them, rather than beat ourselves up.

Examples: "This should never have happened to me." "I must always keep myself calm and together."

Can you think of an example of when you have done this in the past?

_____

_____

_____

_____

Are there any areas of your life where you are doing this now?

_____

_____

_____

_____

What are the situations in which you are most likely to think this way?

_____

_____

_____

_____

CONFIRMATION BIAS

In this type of distorted thinking, once you have an idea in your head, you pay attention to things that support your idea and ignore disconfirming evidence.

> **Example:** If you have been cheated on in the past, you might be suspicious of your current partner. If he becomes less amorous with you, you suspect he is giving his affections to someone else. If he becomes more amorous, you suspect he has been stimulated by someone else. If he acts the same, you suspect he is hiding the fact that he is with someone else. In a sad, self-fulfilling prophecy, your paranoia actually drives a wedge in the relationship, making it more likely he will want to find someone else.

Can you think of an example of when you have done this in the past?

_____

_____

_____

Are there any areas of your life where you are doing this now?

_____

_____

_____

What are the situations in which you are most likely to think this way?

_____

_____

_____

OLD, OBSOLETE, OR INAPPROPRIATE THINKING

There are countless other unhelpful thinking patterns that can develop. Perhaps they were helpful in the past, or even now in certain situations.

> **Example:** If you work in a job in which other businesses call you all day trying to sell you things, being cynical and putting up walls can help protect you from making bad purchases. But if you come home and are automatically cynical and defensive with your family, your relationships will suffer.

Can you think of an example of when you have done this in the past?

_____

_____

_____

_____

Are there any areas of your life where you are doing this now?

_____

_____

_____

_____

What are the situations in which you are most likely to think this way?

_____

_____

_____

_____

Uncovering
Core Beliefs

Both consciously and subconsciously, our brains are continuously being programmed by the words, opinions, and beliefs of our families, friends, authority figures, and the broader society in which we live. Some of this programming is desirable and good, but some programming is quite negative, having the effect of putting you down or making you feel less than you really are. This is a normal and natural part of growing up and learning to fit into society, but many of us incorporate these beliefs so deeply that we barely notice them. Known as "core beliefs," they are patterns of thinking with which we have become so identified that we rarely question them.

Some of these beliefs may be positive, such as a deep belief that we are worth being loved and that life is good. However, many people uncover negative core beliefs like, "I don't deserve to be happy," or "No one can be trusted," perhaps due to past mistreatment, or due to well-meaning but misguided elders and "betters." If deep down, you do not believe you deserve to be happy, you will probably sabotage the attempts of others, and even your own attempts, to foster more happiness in your life.

Take some time to ponder the questions below deeply. Sit with each one for a while. Ideally, you could work with just one question each day. Repeat the question to yourself all throughout the day, letting it percolate in the back of your mind. Watch what comes up for you, and write down your observations. Consider how each core belief impacts you or has impacted you in the past. Note how the same core belief may sometimes be helpful, and may sometimes be harmful. It might also be useful to come back and repeat this exercise once in a while, to see how your core beliefs shift over time.

SELF
Deep down, what do you believe about yourself?

_____

_____

_____

_____

What feelings come up with, or are attached to, these beliefs?

_____

_____

_____

_____

_____

How have these beliefs affected you in the past?

_____

_____

_____

How do these beliefs affect you now?

_____

_____

_____

RELATIONSHIPS

Deep down, what do you believe about relationships with other people? Are people basically good or bad? Can people be trusted?

_____

_____

_____

_____

_____

What feelings come up with, or are attached to, these beliefs?

_____

_____

_____

How have these beliefs affected you in the past?

_____

_____

_____

How do these beliefs affect you now?

_____

_____

_____

WORLD

Deep down, what do you believe about the world? Is it a safe place? How connected do you feel to the environment and the greater universe around you?

_____

_____

_____

_____

_____

What feelings come up with, or are attached to, these beliefs?

_____

_____

_____

How have these beliefs affected you in the past?

_____

_____

_____

How do these beliefs affect you now?

_____

_____

_____

LIFE

Deep down, what do you believe about life? What do you believe constitutes "the good life"? Does life have meaning or purpose? How do you feel about determinism versus free will? What do you believe will happen when you die?

_____

_____

_____

_____

_____

What feelings come up with, or are attached to, these beliefs?

_____

_____

_____

How have these beliefs affected you in the past?

_____

_____

_____

How do these beliefs affect you now?

_____

_____

_____

OTHER CORE BELIEFS

What other deeply held beliefs do you hold?

_____

_____

_____

What feelings come up with, or are attached to, these beliefs?

_____

_____

_____

How have these beliefs affected you in the past?

_____

_____

_____

How do these beliefs affect you now?

_____

_____

_____

❧

The point of this exercise is not necessarily to force yourself to think more positively, but simply to notice deeply ingrained patterns of thinking that might be affecting your experience of life. These beliefs were likely laid down over many years, so if you find some that you wish to change, remember that doing so may take some patient reprogramming.

Part 3

Mindfulness Tools

Jon Kabat-Zinn defines mindfulness as, "The awareness that emerges, through paying attention, in a particular way, on purpose, in the present moment, nonjudgmentally, to the unfolding of experience from moment to moment."

Now, let's explore this definition in depth by examining it line by line. Doing this will not only deepen your own understanding of mindfulness, but allow you to offer clients a more nuanced and precise description of it.

The Awareness That Emerges

Many times throughout the day, we get lost in our heads, then suddenly, we "wake up," and our awareness emerges into where we are right now. Many of us spend much of our lives on "automatic pilot," barely aware of what we are doing. On autopilot, we miss the richness of even the mundane events in our daily lives, and might even later wish for those "good old days" when our kids were younger, because we were not really present as they were growing up.

Sometimes we operate on a literal automatic pilot. Have you ever been driving your car, lost in your thoughts, then suddenly, you find yourself pulling into your own driveway, wondering how you got there? Somehow, you navigated through the traffic, and stopped at all the stoplights, and yet you never really noticed what you were doing. It can sometimes be helpful to do things automatically, but it can also get us into trouble. I was once giving a friend a ride home, but got so caught up in our conversation that I ended up automatically driving to my own house!

As we all know from our psychotherapy work, becoming clearly aware of what is really going on is one of the biggest factors in helping people get better. In organizational consultation work, very often just clearly defining the problems and clarifying the dynamics involved is an intervention all by itself (Sears, Rudisill, & Mason-Sears, 2006). Once people accurately perceive a situation, they are in a much better place to decide if or how they want to change things if they can. To clearly perceive, people must have the capacity to pay attention.

Through Paying Attention

If you remember nothing else about what mindfulness is, "paying attention" is an excellent, succinct definition. In fact, some of the early research on mindfulness called it "attentional control training" (Teasdale, Segal, & Williams, 1995).

Mindfulness practices directly exercise our capacity to pay attention. When you notice your mind wandering, you bring it back to where you want it to be. When it wanders off again, you simply bring it back yet again. When you repeatedly use specific brain circuits, like those used in attention, those circuits begin to build up and become stronger and more efficient. This principle is known as "Hebb's Rule," which can be summarized as "neurons that fire together, wire together" (Hebb, 1949). We'll see later in the book that certain areas of the brain actually get measurably thicker after just eight weeks of mindfulness training.

You might naturally ask, "Should I pay attention all the time?" For one thing, there is simply too much to pay attention to in any given moment. Trying to pay attention to everything all the time would simply wear you out.

In a Particular Way

This part of the definition has to do with the attitude that develops with mindfulness practice, which may sound a bit strange at first. The attitude is one of interest, curiosity, and kindness toward one's own experiences, even during difficult times. On the five-factor personality scale, this quality is known as "openness to experience" (Costa & Widiger, 2002).

Instead of trying to "control" our thoughts, emotions, and body sensations, which leads to a lifelong sense of struggle, mindfulness practice teaches us to become kinder to ourselves. We begin to let go of the struggle. Instead of getting caught up in thoughts, we note, "thoughts about being a terrible person are here." Instead of getting overly caught up in the emotions, we notice, "anxiety is present right now." By stepping back, we get perspective on our thoughts and emotions, and make more conscious choices about how to respond to situations.

On Purpose

Mindfulness is a conscious, intentional activity, and differs in this respect from hypnosis, relaxation exercises, and other forms of meditation. Since mindfulness simply means paying attention, it will never tell you what to do. It is up to you to choose where you want to place your attention.

There are no "shoulds" in mindfulness. If right now, you were thinking about other things and having a hard time paying attention to what you were reading, I would not tell you that you should stop thinking about other things and pay attention to my words. If I were there, I would simply ask you, "Are you thinking about those other things on purpose?" Perhaps you have a family member in crisis right now, and you need to think of a plan to help them. In that case, I would recommend putting this book down and focusing on making that plan. However, it is more likely that you would tell me that you just keep thinking about work, and you do not want to be thinking about work right now. In that case, I would suggest you practice putting your attention where you want your attention to be. Of course, that takes practice.

The important question here is, "How is this working for me?" If something is not going the way you want it to be going, awareness is a good tool to have.

In the Present Moment

The only time that you will ever do anything, feel anything, or experience anything is in the present moment. However, in our minds, many of us are constantly somewhere else, often in the past or the future. Someone once sent me a comic strip cartoon that illustrates this point. In the first square, it showed a man at work, with a thought bubble showing that he was thinking about playing golf. In the next square, he was playing golf, but thinking about sex. In the final square, it showed him having sex, but with a thought bubble indicating that he was thinking about work.

In mindfulness exercises, we practice bringing our attention back to this present moment. Of course, mind-wandering is natural, and this sometimes leads to new and creative ideas. But when we find ourselves endlessly lost in mental realms that are not relevant to our lives, we can choose more often to bring our attention into the present.

The past only exists in your memory. The future only exists in your thinking. When you recognize that the present moment is all that there is, you can feel a sense of vast openness about the now. While this may sound a little philosophical at first, you can experience this for yourself when you pay attention and suspend the compulsive judgment of the thinking mind.

Nonjudgmentally

Fostering a nonjudgmental attitude does not mean that we get rid of using discernment to determine whether or not something is good or bad for us, to decide what might be helpful or harmful to others, or to compare how things are now with how we want them to be.

In mindfulness practice, nonjudgmentally really means temporarily suspending, or setting aside, our constant, habitual, compulsive tendency to judge, or compare, this moment with some other time or some other place.

If you are kissing your partner, and the whole time you are thinking to yourself, "This kiss is okay, but the kiss she gave me yesterday was spectacular! Why won't she kiss me like that?" Obviously, while you are thinking that, you are not actually feeling the kiss taking place in that moment. When you can set aside the filter of comparisons, you can experience your moments much more directly, and they become much more vivid and fulfilling.

To the Unfolding of Experience Moment to Moment

Sometimes I meet people who think mindfulness is always about peace and stillness, almost with an attitude of, "Nobody move, I want to be mindful!"

Mindfulness is an active, dynamic process. Even though we might regularly practice mindfulness while sitting still, the point is to bring greater awareness into more of the experiences of our daily lives, such as our relationships and our work, whether those moments are fun or extremely challenging.

As a mental health professional, not only will clients appreciate you being more present with them, but you will also reduce your own stress levels if you can keep your attention on the moment you are in. No matter what else you have to do later, no matter how many phone calls you have to make, or reports you have to write, you cannot do them when you are with a client.

Plus, Acceptance

Acceptance is very related to the concept of nonjudgment, and it tends to be just as misunderstood. Normally, when we say, "I accept that," there is an implication that you are sort of okay with it. In the mindfulness context, however, you may *not* be okay with it. You may be experiencing a horrible tragedy, and might not like it at all.

Acceptance does not mean resignation. It does not mean that you just curl up in a ball and feel completely hopeless. You may well do everything in your power in the next moment to make things different if you can, but there is no way you can do or fix anything if you cannot get in touch with the way things are right now.

When we let go of our struggles with our present moment experiences, even if they are painful, we can use that energy to consciously build a life worth living.

MINDFUL INQUIRY

Processing a mindfulness exercise with clients immediately afterward is called mindful inquiry (Kabat-Zinn, 2013; Sears, 2015; Segal, Williams, & Teasdale, 2013; Woods, 2013), which is arguably even more important than doing the exercise itself. You never know for certain what clients are actually doing in their heads during a mindfulness exercise, so processing it with them models the skills and attitudes that you want them to eventually internalize for themselves. In the MBCT protocol, for example, we typically ask clients three questions after introducing a new mindfulness exercise.

The first question is simply, "What did you notice during that exercise?" The therapist encourages clients to pay attention to their thoughts, emotions, body sensations, and other sensory experiences. The therapist models acceptance and nonjudgment by responding in a similar way to all clients, regardless of whether they had a "good" or "bad" experience. When follow up questions are asked, they invite the clients to look more deeply into their own experiences. For example, if clients say they fell asleep, the therapist might ask how they knew they fell asleep, what the first signs of sleepiness were, or what thoughts, emotions, and/or body sensations were present.

The second question is basically, "How is what you just did different from the way you normally do things?" This highlights awareness of what the client was doing differently during the exercise, so that they realize that by consciously doing something different, they can have a different experience.

The third question is where the rubber meets the road. "Why do you think we're doing this? What's the practical value? How can you use this in your daily life? How can an exercise like this help your stress, anxiety, depression, pain, or whatever it is you came here for?" Most clients are already thinking this, especially the first few times they practice mindfulness, so it is best to make the question explicit. Since clients know their own lives better than the therapist does, they often come up with creative and powerful ways in which they can apply the material. Also, from a social psychology perspective, if clients come up with their own reasons for doing the exercises, they are more likely to try them. Telling clients they need to do something because it is good for them often fosters resistance, as well as implies that they have to get rid of uncomfortable experiences, thoughts, or feelings right away. Staying present with whatever they bring up helps them viscerally experience the nonjudgmental attitude of acceptance of how things are in the moment. It is just about noticing.

This is especially true for the clients who are the most vocal in the early sessions with complaints like, "I have REAL pain, I've got REAL problems! How is sitting here supposed to help with all the things I have to deal with?!" Time and time again, these clients are the ones who at the end of an eight-week mindfulness program will say, "Thank you so much for staying present with me through all my complaints, and all my emotional ups and downs, because you taught me how to do that for myself."

That is the power of mindful inquiry.

The worksheet that follows can be useful for both you and your clients to practice the skills of mindful inquiry after an exercise.

Mindful Inquiry
and Practice Log

Use this worksheet to process the mindfulness exercises you are practicing. Since mindfulness is about paying attention, working through these questions will deepen your capacity to be present with your own experiences. It can also serve as a record of how your experiences and insights change over time. **A number of free mindfulness recordings are available online, including the author's website, www.psych-insights.com/mindfulness**

Circle which mindfulness exercise(s) you did:

Body Scan	Breath	Entire Body	Seeing
Hearing	3-Minute Breathing Space	Working with a Difficulty	Choiceless Awareness
Walking	Yoga	Loving-kindness	Other_____

What did you notice during the exercise?

_____

_____

_____

_____

What thoughts were present?

_____

_____

_____

_____

How did they change over the course of the exercise?

_____

_____

_____

_____

What emotions were present?

_____

_____

_____

_____

How and where did you experience the emotions in your body?

_____

_____

_____

_____

Did the emotions change over time? If so, in what way?

_____

_____

_____

_____

What physical sensations did you notice?

_____

_____

_____

_____

How did the physical sensations change over the course of the exercise?

_____

_____

_____

_____

What did you notice with your other senses (seeing, hearing, smelling, tasting)?

_____

_____

_____

_____

Did you notice interactions between your thoughts, emotions, body sensations, and/or sensory experiences?

_____

_____

_____

_____

What else did you notice about this exercise?

_____

_____

_____

_____

Did you experience anything differently during this exercise as compared to how you normally operate in your daily life?

_____

_____

_____

_____

Are there ways that you can apply the practice you just did to enrich your daily life?

_____

_____

_____

_____

What thoughts, emotions, or body sensations are you noticing right now, in this moment, after answering the questions?

_____

_____

_____

_____

COMMITTING TO PURPOSE AND VALUES

Mindfulness is about noticing things as they are in this moment, which allows clients to begin to let go of their internal struggles with their own experiences. However, the million-dollar question that comes up is, what do you want to do with your life? What is important to you?

Acceptance and Commitment Therapy or ACT (pronounced as one word, to emphasize taking action), helps clients find their own answers to these important questions. ACT is an evidenced-based intervention with a great deal of research support which builds on the foundations of behavioral and cognitive therapies. This approach uses mindfulness and acceptance processes to help clients let go of unnecessary struggle, and behavioral change processes to help clients live a more fulfilling life.

Understandably, clients often get so stuck in dealing with their problems, and so caught up in their thoughts and emotions, that they forget to live. Clients often persist in the same behaviors, hoping to achieve different results.

Rather than aiming at symptom reduction, ACT is about helping clients identify and move toward what is most important to them. They are then asked if they would be willing to commit to moving toward those values, even if their unpleasant experiences do not go away.

If I had tried to sell you on the experience of graduate school, would it have sounded very appealing? "Have I got a deal for you! When you enter graduate school, you will give up several years of your life, get into so much debt that you could have bought a house with that money, experience high levels of stress that might lead to health problems, become sleep deprived, and you might even lose a significant relationship or two along the way. How does that sound?"

While hopefully you managed to also enjoy your life during graduate school, you endured the stress because you had a bigger value that inspired you, that of living the glamorous lifestyle of a mental health professional.

Think about the clients with whom you have worked who have been most successful. Chances are, they had some bigger reason why they were motivated to get better.

ACT teaches clients that thoughts and feelings do not have to drive your life. Through acceptance and defusion processes, clients learn to recognize their internal experiences for what they are, and consciously decide what actions to take based on their values rather than based solely on a need to avoid unpleasant thoughts and emotions.

Sadly, many clients have great difficulty shifting from surviving to living, and have a lot of trouble identifying what they value. The first worksheet can help spark the process of getting in touch with values, and the second gives a "bus metaphor" for taking committed action. Of course, as human beings ourselves, this is also important for us as therapists to practice in our own lives.

Identifying Your Values

As a young child, do you remember what you wanted to be when you grew up? Most children have lots of dreams, and don't even worry about how they will make them happen. However, as we grow up, well-intentioned parents and teachers advise us to be "practical." The older we get, the more we limit our dreams. Eventually, many people focus only on daily problems, and forget what is most important in life. When life becomes nothing but surviving and dealing with problems, it turns into drudgery. Many people forget how to truly live. For example, a lot of people work to get money to support their families, but end up working so much that they never spend much time with their families, and are left feeling depressed when the children grow up and move away.

Getting in touch with what we truly value reminds us of what life is all about. Our values give our lives direction. No matter how challenging our problems get, our values serve as compass headings, reminding us of what is really important.

No one can tell you what your values are. As you begin to explore what they might be for you, watch out for old programming from parents or society telling you what "should" be important. A value is something you just feel pulled to do.

Values fall into broad categories, like family, spirituality, learning, adventure, or creativity. You never "arrive" at a value. For example, family is something that you are always moving toward. You are never "done" with family. However, it is important to set more specific goals to guide you in the direction of family, like getting out of your house, going on dates, etc. Goals may shift with time, but they keep you going in the direction of your values.

If you are accustomed to only focusing on daily survival, it will take some practice to wake up the creative parts of your brain. Your internal editor will quickly shut down many of your ideas as "impractical. "You can think about how practical you want to be later. For now, just let yourself dream a little to wake up those long-dormant parts of yourself. Go back over this worksheet from time to time, and your values will become more and more clear for you.

When you were a kid, what were some of the things you wanted to be when you grew up?

_____

_____

_____

_____

Imagine you could fast forward into the future toward the end of your life. What would you want your obituary to say? What would have constituted a life well lived?

_____

_____

_____

_____

If you did not have to worry about money, time, or any other obstacle, what would you want to do with your life? How would you want to spend your time? What would make your life meaningful?

_____

_____

_____

_____

Given your answers to the above questions, what values are beginning to come up for you? What is really important to you?

_____

_____

_____

_____

What are some concrete goals can you set to move yourself in the direction of your values?

_____

_____

_____

_____

What steps can you take today to move toward what is important to you? Tomorrow? Next week? Next month? Next year?

_____

_____

_____

_____

_____

The ACT Bus

Many people get stuck in "survival mode." They spend so much of their time and energy earning a living and dealing with their problems that they forget how to live, much less how to thrive. Too often, they tell themselves, "As soon as all these problems are fixed, my to-do list is taken care of, and things settle down for me, then I'm going to start living and enjoying my life." Unfortunately, if that is your attitude, you may just run out of lifetime before that ever really happens. The important thing is to move toward your values, even if you are suffering right now.

Acceptance and Commitment Therapy uses a bus metaphor to illustrate how we lose touch with where we are going in life. You are the driver of your bus, which represents your life. As you grow older, you take on a lot of passengers, which represent your life experiences, memories, thoughts, and feelings. Some of these passengers are pleasant, and some of them are downright monstrous. The monstrous ones tend to be very loud and bothersome, shouting, screaming, and throwing spitballs at you. Sometimes people get into intense arguments with these monsters, or try to throw them off the bus, but that only tends to make them louder and stronger.

Because these monsters are so obnoxious, people start doing things to appease them more. When they start driving the bus toward their values, the monsters scream and get really rowdy, so they decide not to go that way anymore. They end up only driving in very narrow patterns, because they don't want to upset the monsters too much.

When you realize the pattern you have gotten stuck in, you have only two choices. You can choose to keep trying to avoid upsetting the monsters by keeping your life narrowly confined. It does work in the short run, which is why so many people do it, but it does not lead to a very fulfilling life. The other option is to choose to take control of your bus, and go where you want to go, even if the monsters yell and scream at you the entire time.

What monsters are on your bus? What thoughts, emotions, or body sensations try to control your choices and actions?

_____

_____

_____

_____

When do your monsters get the noisiest? What makes them get rowdy?

_____

_____

_____

_____

What do they shout at you?

_____

_____

_____

_____

What have you given up by trying not to upset the monsters? In what ways has your life become more restricted?

_____

_____

_____

_____

The monsters are scary, but you are the one sitting behind the steering wheel and directing your life. Thoughts and feelings can't control your actions. Where do you want to drive your bus, even if the monsters yell at you? What life directions or values are so important to you that you would be willing to bring the monsters with you if you had to?

_____

_____

_____

_____

❧

In any given moment, you can check in with what is happening. Then ask yourself, "Is what I'm doing bringing me closer to the things I value, or farther away?" You certainly don't have to move toward your values all the time, but if you can check your compass every now and then, it will prevent you from going in circles or getting lost. Remember to ask yourself, "Who's driving my bus? Me, or the monsters?" You are perfectly at liberty to go where the monsters tell you, but if you don't like where that takes you, remember that you always have the choice to steer back to where you want to go. It doesn't matter where you've been. You can always set a new course in each moment.

If you keep doing what you've always done, you will keep getting what you've always got. Moving toward your values requires committed action. Toward that end, ask yourself the following questions:

Can I make a commitment to myself to move toward what is important to me?

_____

_____

_____

Am I willing to experience uncomfortable thoughts and feelings if I can live a richer life? Am I willing to try something new in order to get something new?

_____

_____

_____

❧

Be careful not to let your thoughts and feelings, your "monsters," decide for you. Either you choose to act or you choose not to. You cannot "try" to jump. You either jump or you don't. It doesn't matter if you jump an inch or ten feet. The important thing is to jump in the direction of what you value.

EXPOSURE TO INTERNAL EXPERIENCES

While we will discuss details about exposure therapy in Part 4, Tools for Stress and Anxiety Disorders, one of the ways mindfulness can be clinically useful is as a tool for exposing clients to their own internal experiences (thoughts, emotions, and body sensations). This counters unhealthy experiential avoidance and fosters psychological flexibility, which frees the client to take action toward a more fulfilling life (Hayes, Strosahl, & Wilson, 2012).

Naturally, no one wants to feel uncomfortable, so whatever lessens an unpleasant emotion can get negatively reinforced. Clients who feel anxiety, for example, tend to go off into a mental realm of thoughts and images, worrying or ruminating. While clients are in their heads, they are less acutely aware of the physical sensations in their bodies, and therefore experience reduced anxiety, negatively reinforcing their thinking. **Instead of getting lost in thoughts, clients can learn to shift attention to the physical sensations, a kind of exposure therapy to the body. Awareness of the body will increase the experience of anxiety at first (extinction burst), but without avoidance through the distraction of thoughts, the anxiety will often subside in a few minutes.**

I once had a client who had struggled with anxiety for many years. He had read many books, and tried many other therapists, and none of them could take away his anxiety. After getting a good background history, and making sure he had already ruled out medical issues, I decided to have him practice exposure therapy to his own body sensations.

I first asked him how strong his anxiety was on a scale of 1-10, and he replied that it was an "8." When you use a SUDS, or subjective units of distress scale (1-10 or 1-100), I highly recommend asking clients this simple follow-up question. I asked the client, "How do you know it is an 8?" In other words, what information or data is the client basing that number on?

Like most clients, he had no idea at first how to respond to such a question, so I said, "Chances are, there is a place in your body giving you information about how anxious you are."

After a few minutes, he said, "It's in my brain." I informed him that it was not possible to feel anything in your brain tissue, so he was probably confusing a thought with a feeling. I invited him to keep looking for the sensations in his body that were fueling those thoughts.

Finally, he informed me that he was noticing a lot of strong tension in the muscles of his neck. Before I could even say anything, he said, "Huh! I wonder if all these years, I was feeling tension in my neck, and I thought that was anxiety, so I have been anxious about being anxious!"

Moving into our own internal experiences helps us to unpack them. Though they are all interactive with each other, it can be helpful for clients to learn to separate out thoughts, emotions, and body sensations. This gives us three places to intervene.

Tips for Getting Clients into the Body

With notable exceptions, many clinicians are only trained to work with clients' thoughts. I'll bet you can recall working with quite a few clients who were stuck in their thinking, and maybe a specific person comes to your mind. Since you are an experienced professional, after a good intake, you knew exactly what the problem was, so you told the client exactly what to do. But the client replied with, "I tried that before, and it doesn't work!" Since you are probably a polite person, you may have followed up with another helpful suggestion, but the client immediately said, "I tried that too, and that doesn't work either!" After your third suggestion, the client may have said something like, "I tried that six months ago, and it still doesn't work!"

This kind of stalemate often results because you are fighting the client's thoughts with more thoughts. When this occurs, I find it much more useful to drop beneath the thoughts and get to the root source. "I'll bet you're feeling very frustrated right now that nothing has been working." They would not be having those thoughts without an underlying feeling like frustration, so I might invite them to get more in touch with that emotion, and move into the associated body sensations.

Of course, clients rarely understand concepts like negative reinforcement and the importance of exposure. It often makes no sense to them that experiencing an emotion like anxiety more directly in their bodies will help – it's the opposite of common sense. To understand this principle, I have found that clients can relate well to an analogy of moving into a cold swimming pool, which is described in the next handout.

Moving Into
the Swimming Pool

Our emotions can become a huge source of distress for us, but we forget that they are actually designed to simply deliver a message and pass away. A pure, raw, intense emotion should only last about 90 seconds. If your emotion is staying intense, something is keeping it going. Very often, our struggles with what we are feeling, and our ruminating and worrying, fuel the emotions.

Even though some emotions are very strong, fighting with them only tends to make them worse. When we remember that our feelings are trying to give us a message, we can practice feeling them more directly. Even if we don't like the message, if we can receive it, we can let go of the struggle. We can then choose to do what is important in our lives rather than spend all our time fighting or avoiding our feelings.

Moving into our emotions is a lot like going into a cold swimming pool. When you dip your toe into the water and find out that it is a little cold, you might want to stay away. But if you decide you want to go in and spend time with your friends or family, you know you are going to feel colder when you first go in. However, you also know that if you just stay in the water, your body will adjust, and you won't even feel the cold after a little while.

You have basically two options — diving in, or going in slowly. Some people like to cannonball into the pool, and freeze for a minute or two (around 90 seconds, right?), and then they feel fine. Other people like to go over to the steps and go into the pool gradually — putting in the left foot first, and waiting for it to adjust, then putting the right foot into the pool, and waiting for it to adjust, then going in up to the knees, then up to the waist, then up to the chest, then submerging themselves.

However you do it, the important thing is to stay in the water. You will feel worse at first, but your body will adjust. Your emotions, like stress and anxiety, will respond in the very same way. If you feel your emotions directly in the body — your pounding heartbeat, your queasy stomach, your tingling fingertips, the knots in your shoulders — they will get a little worse at first. But if you practice staying with them, they will deliver their messages and start to ease up. The problem is, we tend to jump out of our bodies and into our heads with thoughts, like, "Hmmm, my heart is beating awfully fast. Is it supposed to beat that fast? Maybe something is really wrong with it. Gee, if I keeled over dead right here, that would be so embarrassing! How would my family find out about it? They might go for days without knowing what happened to me. I wonder what kind of funeral I would get? I really should have finished my will. There is just so much paper piled up at home, I really need to clean that up this weekend."

Our thoughts can carry us away so quickly, which creates the same problems as jumping back out of the pool. With practice, we learn to say, "Thank you for trying to help me, brain, but I'm going to just feel the feelings that are here in my body." Of course, you'll feel a little worse at first, which is why your brain keeps trying to tell you that's a bad idea, but just stay with what you feel in your body as best you can.

If you want to enjoy swimming, the worst thing you can do is jump into the pool, then jump out, then jump in, then jump out, over and over again. Unfortunately, this is what most people do with their feelings. They feel them a little, get uncomfortable, then push them away, or just go on and on with worrying and ruminating. Sadly, some people do this their whole lives.

Sometimes people think they can just feel it for a little while, fighting it the whole time, and then get away from it again, and they wonder why that approach doesn't work. That's like jumping into the swimming pool, running as fast as you can to get to the other side, then jumping back out again. Your body doesn't have time to adjust.

It takes a little faith to jump in. It might get very uncomfortable at first. The good news is that the more you do it, the easier it gets. You know that it won't last if you stay in the pool. You know that jumping out might quickly make you feel a little better at first, but it will make the problem worse in the long run.

Most importantly, try to be kind to yourself. If someone you cared about, like a friend or child, was feeling strong emotions like anxiety, you would probably be able to hug them compassionately. Try to hold your own emotions in the same gentle way, no matter how strong they are.

Some people go their whole lives standing on the side of the pool, watching everyone else swimming and having fun, too embarrassed by their fear to move into the initial discomfort of going into the pool. If you fast forward your life to the point when you are on your deathbed, do you think you will wish you had spent more time in the pool or standing on the side?

DECENTERING AND DEFUSION

When thoughts become strong and very negative, clients can become overly identified with their thinking and emotions, and feel themselves to be in the center of them. Thoughts, which are simply internalized words, become "fused" with conditioned meanings and emotions. For example, when I say, "Jack and Jill went up the _____," most English speakers will immediately think "hill." The human brain automatically makes associations. Sometimes they are quite useful, but other times the associations can be blatantly wrong and emotionally painful. A client with depression who thinks, "I'm no good" will likely have all kinds of negative meanings associated with those sounds, and will likely automatically feel sadness with the thought.

Mindfulness teaches clients to "decenter" or "defuse" from their thoughts. Since thoughts are in reality only mental events, clients can learn to experience them as such. For example, an ACT therapist might ask a client to write down a distressing thought like, "I'm a terrible person" onto a piece of paper. The therapist then asks the client to hold the paper up to their face, and asks them how well they can interact with other people and live a very fulfilling life when they are so close to that thought. The client is then asked to place the paper in their lap, and realizes that even if the thought is still present, the client can go on to do meaningful things and engage in their relationships (Hayes, Strosahl, & Wilson, 2012).

When my youngest daughter was three years old, I was driving her home from school one day, and she was uncharacteristically quiet in the back seat. All of a sudden, I heard her say to herself, "Sorry brain, I'm not going to do what you tell me to do." I was impressed by her ability to practice decentering. She had a thought about throwing her doll out the window, and she realized she did not have to engage in that behavior.

Tips for Teaching Defusion

ACT uses the "milk exercise" to teach defusion from thoughts (Hayes, Strosahl, & Wilson, 2012). When you see, hear, or say the word "milk," you probably bring to mind a white, creamy substance. You might imagine the taste, or you might even bring to mind memories of being forced to drink milk when you were a kid. But notice what happens when you repeat the word over and over again. Say the word milk out loud for about 30 seconds. Go ahead and do that before reading further.

What happened? For most people, the sounds become untangled from the automatic associations and emotions. It starts to become nothing but sound, which is all it ever was. Only your brain puts meaning on that word. Of course, thoughts themselves are neither good nor bad. When seen for what it is, thinking can be a very useful tool. When we get overly caught up in thinking, and confuse the conditioned associations with reality, it can cause us great distress.

Of course, being aware of one's own thoughts is a very sophisticated meta-cognitive ability, and can be very challenging for clients. The next handout and worksheet may be helpful for clients to learn decentering and defusion. Since challenging thoughts may lead some clients into more struggle, a typical mindfulness-based thought record differs from a traditional CBT thought record by emphasizing noticing over disputation.

Getting Perspective on Your Thoughts

Have you ever had a thought stuck in your mind? Thoughts seem so real and so powerful. We tend to forget that in reality, thoughts are nothing more than words in our heads. There is not really another person inside there. There is no one to argue with, and no one to win against. If a thought comes up like, "I am a bad person," it can feel so true and so strong, and we can get lost in it. However, we can practice "stepping back" from our thoughts. We can remind ourselves, "I am having a thought that I am a bad person." That thought is not you. Most likely, it is a sign that you are distressed.

Acceptance and Commitment Therapy (ACT) calls this a shift from self-as-content to self-as-context. Instead of feeling like we ARE the content of our thoughts, we can practice recognizing that we HAVE thoughts. You have thoughts, but you are more than just your thinking.

ACT uses a chessboard analogy to illustrate this point. If you identify who you are with your thoughts, it is like identifying with the chess pieces on a chessboard. You get very caught up in which side is going to win, obsess about strategy, get anxious about moves and countermoves, and get upset if you lose. However, without the chessboard, there could not be a chess game. You are more like the chessboard. Without you, there could be no thoughts. The chessboard is not affected at all by the outcome of the game. The board does not care who wins or loses, and is not scarred by the battle.

As with any skill, it takes practice to develop a consistent and reliable ability to get perspective on your thoughts. We are often so fused with our thinking that we don't notice it. For example, if you find yourself thinking, "I'm not having any thoughts right now," that itself is a thought!

Take some time to practice paying attention to your thoughts. To help keep you on track, you can download and follow along with a recording, such as the sitting practice on the author's website (www. psych-insights.com/mindfulness). You can also find a quiet place to sit and allow yourself to notice what is going on in your mind. Begin by taking some deep breaths and settling into a comfortable position. See if you can notice what thoughts are coming and going from moment to moment. When you notice yourself getting caught up in the thoughts, or carried away by them, practice "stepping back" from them. Practice noticing what you are thinking without getting lost in the thoughts.

As you develop some skill with this, you will begin to notice the patterns of thinking that your brain gets caught up in. You will notice that you not only think with words, but often with images and colors. You might begin to notice how even small pieces of thoughts can trigger emotions and body sensations.

Thoughts can be very subtle and hard to notice. For some people, using visual imagery can help them focus in order to better recognize what thoughts are coming and going in their minds. Below are some commonly used analogies, but feel free to invent your own.

MOVIE THEATRE
When we watch a good movie, we feel completely absorbed in it, as if what we are watching is really happening. We get angry or scared, and we laugh or cry, even though in the backs of our minds we know that in reality we are only watching flickering images on a screen, a quick succession of pictures of actors made years ago in other times and places.

Our minds can create some very believable movies, because it has no budget constraints, but we can practice remembering that they are only projections of the mind. Imagine yourself sitting in a movie theatre, able to see your thoughts being projected onto a giant screen in front of you. Patiently watch and notice what thoughts and images appear, linger, and disappear on the screen of the mind. When you notice yourself getting caught up in the action and drama of the thoughts, simply remind yourself that you are watching a movie. When you realize that you have been sucked into the movie, imagine yourself moving back out into the theatre chairs, and simply notice the content on the screen.

WATERFALL
You can also imagine your thoughts as a flowing stream of water, continuously cascading down over you. When you step behind the waterfall, you no longer get wet. You can just watch the thoughts flow past you. Watch for the tendency to get pulled back into the waterfall, and keep practicing stepping behind the thoughts to simply notice them.

THOUGHT TRAINS
In the train analogy, you can imagine your thoughts as trains that are moving through your mind. You may even notice multiple trains of thought in any given moment. When you get caught on one of the

thought trains, you are carried away by it, feeling the wind whipping over you and the jostling of the train. When you notice that happening, you simply imagine rising up above the trains, just watching them as they go by. A few moments later, you will probably get carried away by another thought train. When you notice that you are on another train, just rise up above that one too. Practice noticing the thought trains without getting carried away by them.

LEAVES AND CLOUDS

You can also imagine your thoughts as passing objects, like leaves floating down a stream, or like clouds floating through the sky. Rather than getting caught up in the thoughts, just see them for what they are — passing, transient phenomena. The leaves float down the stream without leaving a trail behind them. The clouds come and go, and do not leave tracks in the sky. Sometimes the sky is full of stormy clouds, and sometimes the sky is completely clear. The clouds are always changing, and the sky is big enough to contain them all without holding onto them and without pushing them away.

WAITING FOR A MOUSE OR A FISH

Have you ever watched a cat waiting to pounce on a mouse or an insect? An experienced cat is not anxious and shaky. The cat simply sits with full awareness, completely still, in front of a mouse hole until the prey shows itself. Likewise, you can patiently watch for your thoughts to arise.

You can also visualize yourself sitting next to a clear, calm, smooth lake. Every now and then, a fish leaps suddenly, then disappears back into the water, sending ripples that spread waves in all directions. Practice patiently watching for these thoughts to arise and pass away, and you might even begin to notice how thoughts trigger other thoughts and emotions that ripple through the mind.

Imagery can sometimes confuse people. After all, using these techniques are really adding thoughts and images to thoughts. They are just tools meant to help you exercise your ability to get perspective on your thoughts. If you do use a visual metaphor, it is usually best to stick with just one of them. Otherwise, you might find yourself in a movie theatre on a train with leaves floating down a cloudy waterfall full of fish and mice, and lose all sense of what thoughts are actually present. With practice, you will be able to let go of the imagery and notice thoughts more directly.

Be patient with yourself. Thoughts can sometimes be very strong, and sometimes be very subtle. With practice, you will get better at noticing your own thoughts more often throughout the day. Unconscious thoughts have a way of impacting our moods and attitudes. Before we can let go of our struggles with distressing thoughts, we need to be able to recognize them clearly.

Mindfulness Thought Record

When a distressing event occurs during your day, use the form below to practice noticing the links between situations, thoughts, emotions, and body sensations. Rather than automatically feeling like you have to "fix" your thoughts, feelings, and experiences, practice just noticing them as they are in the moment. Over time, you will likely notice consistent patterns that keep coming up.

What was the situation? What happened?

_____

_____

_____

_____

_____

What thoughts were present at the time?

_____

_____

_____

_____

_____

What emotions were present at the time?

_____

_____

_____

_____

What body sensations were present at the time?

_____

_____

_____

_____

What thoughts are coming up now, as you are writing about this situation?

_____

_____

_____

_____

What are emotions are present right now?

_____

_____

_____

_____

What are you feeling in your body right now?

_____

_____

_____

_____

If this exercise has brought up uncomfortable feelings or distressing thoughts, what can you do to take care of yourself right now?

_____

_____

_____

_____

FILLING THE ATTENTIONAL CHANNELS VS. AVOIDANCE

From research in the field of cognitive theory, the study of how the brain processes information, we know that the brain has a limited attentional capacity (Pashler, 1998; Swallow & Jiang, 2013). So, if you fill your attentional channels with present-moment experiences, especially sensory experiences, there is literally less room in your brain for worries and ruminations (Segal, Williams, & Teasdale, 2013; Teasdale, Segal, & Williams, 1995).

This concept is one of the factors in how mindfulness practice can be helpful to clients, since it is about noticing present-moment experiences. However, if clients are using mindfulness techniques to avoid feelings, or to try to force them to go away, they may be falling into avoidance. If someone accepts an emotion to get rid of it, it is not really acceptance.

However, if clients find themselves awake at 3am, their minds stuck in cycles of ruminations and worries, they can very easily practice putting their attention into their senses – hearing the sounds around them, noticing the feeling of the sheets on their skin, feeling the breath, etc.

To give a personal example, I was once giving a workshop far from home, and during the lunch break, there was a message on my cell phone from my brother, informing me that my father had passed away. This was not a complete surprise, because he had been diagnosed with pancreatic cancer, but no one was sure how much longer he would live. In that moment, I had a decision to make. While I'm sure everyone would have understood if I cancelled the rest of the workshop, I realized that I couldn't even get a flight home in the next couple of hours, and my siblings were already there to take care of things. Since there were about 50 mental health professionals in the audience who had all cleared their schedules just for my workshop, I decided to just go ahead and finish the last three hours.

That afternoon, I found it very useful to practice bringing my attention into each moment. To be sure, there were moments when some emotions came up, and I would notice them, but then I would just keep bringing my attention back to the people I was with, and to the material that I was talking about.

Of course, if that was all I ever did, and I never processed my grief, that would be avoidance, and it would have created problems for me down the road.

Isn't it funny that even mindfulness techniques can be used as a form of avoidance in some situations? How do you know when it is helpful and when it might be avoidance? Well, that's why you make the "big bucks" as a mental health professional. It is important to look at the unique circumstances of each individual client. When you understand the principles of avoidance and exposure, you can look at the context and function of the behaviors to determine whether or not they are working for the client.

The next worksheet may be helpful for clients to understand the usefulness of putting their attention into the present moment.

Just this Moment

Have you ever woken up first thing in the morning, and looked at your planner, or just started thinking about all the things you had to deal with that day? Before you even leave your bedroom, your mind is filled with all the people you need to see, the work you have to do, the coworkers you have to deal with, and all the problems that need to be solved. You feel your stress level rise, and you begin to think, "Oh no, this is going to be such a long day!"

However, all those things are only happening in your head. In that moment, you are still just in your bedroom. I certainly hope your coworkers are not really there in your bedroom first thing in the morning! This is the perfect time to practice reminding yourself to come back to the moment you are in. Even if you have a super busy day, you will only be in one moment at a time, and you can only do one thing at a time. You will get out of bed. In another moment, you will walk to the bathroom. In the next moment, you will be eating breakfast. In another moment, you will be driving to work. When you are in a meeting, you are just in that meeting, not yet in the other ones you will have later that day. If you can just stay in each moment as it is happening, it is much less stressful than trying to carry your whole day around in your head all day long. Some people even carry their whole lives around in their heads, with all the worries and regrets they've collected over the years.

The reality is, you will always be in this present moment. Many of us are continuously thinking about the past and the future, but those things only exist in your mind. It can be useful to sometimes learn from the past, and to plan for the future, but living there and constantly worrying keeps the stress response going. Do not forget that this moment is the only thing there is. The only time you will ever feel anything, experience anything, or do anything is in the present moment, which you are in right now.

Whenever you feel like you are lost in your mind, you can practice coming to your senses. Ask yourself what you see, hear, feel, smell, or taste, right now in this moment. Look around you, and see the shapes and colors. Listen to the sounds coming to your ears from both near and far. Notice any feelings in your body, like your breath, your clothing, or the feeling of the chair you are sitting in. Notice any smells in the air. Notice the taste of your food when you are eating.

Right now, in this moment, write down what you see, hear, feel, smell, and taste:

_____

_____

_____

_____

_____

Your brain can only pay attention to so many things in any one given moment. If you fill your brain with what is happening right now, you will get less caught up in unhelpful worrying.

Of course, your problems will not go away. You will still need to deal with some serious things in your life. But worrying about them all day long will not help. If you practice bringing yourself back into the moment, your mind will be more calm and clear, and you will be better able to handle the things you really do have to deal with.

If you find it helpful, write down a list of what you need to worry about. Prioritize the most important things. If there is something you can do right now, you might choose to go ahead and do it. If not, you can just practice noticing what is happening in this moment.

_____

_____

_____

_____

_____

_____

Part 4

Tools for Stress and Anxiety Disorders

Stress and anxiety are very common presenting issues in mental health work. Anxiety disorders include phobias, generalized anxiety disorder, obsessive-compulsive disorder, health anxiety, obsessive-compulsive disorder, panic disorder, posttraumatic stress disorder, panic disorder, and eating disorders. Physiologically, anxiety is basically an overreaction of the stress response system, so we will begin with stress.

THOUGHTS FOR CLINICIANS

Chances are, that for pretty much every client you will ever see, their issues will have at least some stress component, given that most people report feeling at least some stress on a daily basis (American Psychological Association, 2016). In fact, even in primary care physician visits, stress is a factor in up to 80% of the presenting issues (Avey, Matheny, Robbins, & Jacobson, 2003). Stress alone does not cause disease (no one ever developed bubonic plague just from being stressed). However, it can interfere with immune functioning, which leaves a person more vulnerable to getting a disease that comes along, interrupts the person's ability to recover from a disease, or becomes over-stimulated and attacks the person's own body (American Psychological Association, 2012; Sapolsky, 2009; 2010).

In the client handout following, when a threat is perceived, the stress reaction triggers the brain to release glucocorticoids, creating a cascade of effects (Sapolsky, Romero, & Munck, 2000). In addition to helping clients reduce their current levels of stress, it is important to encourage them to attend to their long-term self-care. No matter what the client's main presenting issue, helping them reduce and manage their own stress will be very important for them to improve their daily functioning and to help them live a more fulfilling life. Preventing and managing stress is, of course, also very important for clinicians.

It is important for clients to understand that the stress response itself is simply the body performing a useful, natural function. As we know from the research of Hans Selye (1976), the goal is to find balance, not to eliminate stress. Typically, performance suffers when stress is too high, but with too little stress, performance also suffers due to lack of energy and motivation.

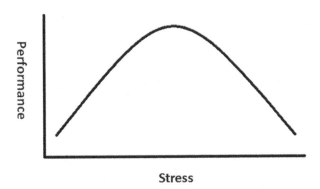

The next handout also discusses the classic social psychology experiment that demonstrates the impact of thinking on the interpretation of the stress response (Aronson, 2012; Schachter & Singer, 1962). Given that a large factor in the stress response is related to thinking, a number of mindfulness programs have been shown to be helpful, such as Mindfulness-Based Stress Reduction, Mindfulness-Based Cognitive Therapy, and Acceptance and Commitment Therapy. Such approaches emphasize relating differently to stress rather than eliminating it. They teach clients how to let go of automatic patterns of mental and physical struggle with the body's stress response. They also emphasize creating a meaningful life, even if that life sometimes contains stressful experiences.

The following handouts and worksheets explain the nature of stress, discuss the interaction of breathing and stress, encourage clients to discover and recognize their personal signs of stress, and provide a template to start building a stress reduction action plan. These handouts will likely be useful for any client, regardless of the primary presenting issue.

The Good and the Bad
of the Stress Response

Everyone experiences high levels of stress at some point in their lives, and many people experience it every day. Wouldn't it be great if nothing ever went wrong in our lives, and everyone around us treated us the way we wanted them to treat us all the time? Meanwhile, back in reality, we cannot escape stress, so it is important to learn how to work with it.

Though it may be funny to think about, we actually do not want to get rid of all stress, even if that would be possible. Stress itself is just energy in response to a situation. When it is too high, it obviously creates problems, but if you actually had no stress, you would feel no energy or motivation to even get out of bed. For example, if you have to take an important test, we all know that too much stress about it will interfere with your concentration and your performance. However, if you felt zero stress about the test, you would not care about how you performed, so you wouldn't bother studying, and you wouldn't try very hard to do well. The goals are to find a balance, to learn how to harness the energy of stress, and to let it go when it gets too high.

The stress response is your body's natural way to help you get ready to deal with something important. If a hungry tiger suddenly jumped out in front of you, your stress response would help save your life, motivating you to flee, fight, or freeze in a hiding place. Your brain would release chemicals like cortisol and adrenaline, which trigger the survival response. You would breathe faster to get more oxygen into your bloodstream. Your heartbeat and blood pressure would go up, transporting that oxygen to your muscles more quickly. Your muscles would tense up to get ready for action. Your digestion would shut down so you would have more energy for your muscles. Your immune system would kick up in case you got injured.

As soon as the tiger threat was gone, your body would reverse the process by kicking in the relaxation response. Your breathing and heart rate would slow down, your muscles would relax, and your digestion would go back to normal.

Here's the problem today. Our brains can conjure up all sorts of imaginary "tigers" with our thinking, and the body responds with the same stress response, albeit a scaled down version. Stuck in traffic? Your brain squirts out some stress chemicals to try to "help" you deal with the situation. Worried about what your boss might say at work today? Another little squirt. Watching the evening news? Probably lots of small squirts during that program.

If our brains are firing up the stress response all throughout the day, and we don't make time for the relaxation response to get activated, all those things that were good in the short term become problems in the long term. We end up with tense muscles, heart problems, digestion issues, or other medical problems.

Here's the kicker. In the moment, you might not actually be in a very stressful situation, but if you are thinking about stressful things, the stress response might just fire a little bit. If we are prone to worrying all day long, stress chemicals can keep firing even when we are in a safe place. The brain can be our worst enemy as well as our best friend.

Our thoughts play a huge role in how we experience the stress response. In a classic study, researchers gave their subjects a shot, and told them that it contained vitamins. In reality, the shot was epinephrine, an artificial form of adrenalin. The subject then went into a room to fill out paperwork with another "subject," who in reality was a confederate working for the researcher. When the confederate acted irritable, subjects later reported that they too felt irritable. When the confederate acted happy, the subjects later reported that they too felt happy. The same body sensations were interpreted as either irritation or happiness depending on the person next to them.

Interestingly, when other research subjects were told the "vitamin shot" had side effects of increased heartbeat and jittery feelings, they were not affected much by the other people in the room, because they had the thought that what was going on in their bodies was due to the shot.

Understanding stress is an important first step in working with it more effectively. Many of us tend to get stressed out about our stress, and the struggle ends up making it worse. Keep in mind that it is your body trying to help. Since there are causes that create the stress response, we can learn to prevent it, and can learn how to activate the relaxation response.

Breathing and Stress

When you notice that your stress is high, a simple, reliable technique to take the edge off is to take some deep breaths. Breathing is intimately tied to the stress response system. When you need to run or fight, you breathe faster to get more oxygen to your muscles. The balance of oxygen and carbon dioxide tells your brain how fast you need to breathe. When you consciously slow down your breathing, your brain kicks up what is known as the body's innate "relaxation response"—automatically lowering pulse rate, respiration, and blood pressure. Likewise, breathing from the diaphragm, or "belly breathing," triggers the vagus nerve, which tells your brain to stop making the stress chemicals and to go back to normal operations.

Also, putting your attention on the breath helps you focus on this moment, instead of getting lost in thoughts about the past or the future. All those anxious thoughts make the brain think it is in danger, and it produces even more stress chemicals.

As funny as it sounds, it can be very helpful to practice breathing. It is ideal to start practicing in a calm, quiet place, but you can do it anywhere, anytime, because as long as you're alive, you'll have your breath with you.

To begin, put one palm on your belly and the other on your chest, so you can distinguish the difference between thinking about your breath and actually feeling it. Take a moment right now to check in with your breathing, and ask yourself the following questions:

- What do you notice about your breathing?
- Is it flowing freely, or are you holding your breath sometimes?
- How quickly are you breathing?
- How deep are your breaths?
- Are you breathing more from the chest or from the belly?

Experiment with taking slower, deeper breaths. Don't push it — you can do it very gradually. If you notice you are taking only two seconds to inhale and two seconds to exhale, see if you can take three seconds each way. Some people say they feel light-headed when they first start to breathe more deeply, but this is usually because they are not used to breathing this way, and it will pass. If it really concerns you though, feel free to lay down on a couch so you don't have to worry about passing out. (And just to settle your fears, on the very unlikely chance that you do pass out, your brain is designed to automatically return your breathing to normal.)

Breathing is a process that is both conscious and unconscious. You can choose to take a deep breath right now, but when you're not paying attention to your breath, it goes on all by itself.

Many people find this a bit weird at first, or even uncomfortable. Sometimes people who have a history of breathing problems, like asthma, emphysema, or COPD, tell me, "I don't want to feel my breath. It freaks me out!"

But you know what? You're going to be breathing for the rest of your life. Making efforts not to feel it only tends to make it worse. In fact, the anxiety about not feeling it ironically makes it more likely that you will have a breathing attack in the future. The good news is that if you just keep letting yourself feel the breath, and just let the stress or anxiety do whatever it wants to do, even though it might feel worse at first, both your breath and your anxiety will eventually settle down. After you practice this a few times, you no longer have to worry about thinking about the breath.

If you're feeling stress or anxiety right now, focus more on the out-breath, with a sense of letting go, like you feel when you sink down into a comfortable chair. You are breathing out the exhaust gases, making room for fresh oxygen. You can even imagine your stressful thoughts and anxiety feelings floating away from you on the breath.

If you're feeling down, or sluggish, or tired, you might choose to focus more on the in-breath. Deeply breathe in the oxygen from the air, and let it deliver its energy to all the parts of your body.

You may be thinking, "I have very real, serious problems in my life. How is breathing going to help?" You don't have to believe me. You don't even have to think it is working as you're doing it. The changes are happening at the cellular level in your body. Just do it and watch what happens. Most people feel at least a little better right away, but keep in mind that doing it once for a few minutes may not make much difference. Be sure to try it for a while before you give up. After all, you are beginning to change many years of old habits.

Breathing itself is pretty easy. The hardest part is to remember to remember to pay attention to your breath more often throughout your busy day. Some people find it helpful to use an app, or set their phones, to randomly sound a soft "ding" to remind them to stop and breathe. The good news is that even if you just pause and take a deep breath a few times a day, you will begin to interrupt that "go-go-go" feeling that many of us have from constant stress. Like any other skill, it gets easier with practice. Eventually, you will find that slower, deeper, belly breathing is actually much more natural than quick, shallow, chest breathing, and it will become a new unconscious habit.

Of course, breathing alone won't fix the practical problems in your life. But when your stress feels less overwhelming, and you are more centered in the present moment, you are going to have a lot more time and energy to focus on creatively dealing with problems as they arise. You'll also be more open to notice the many positive things that you normally take for granted. As Jon Kabat-Zinn says, *"as long as you are breathing, there is more right with you than wrong with you."*

Recognizing When You Are Getting Overwhelmed

Most people don't notice their stress until it become overwhelming. However, unless a major crisis suddenly pops up, it's rare to go from perfectly fine to completely overwhelmed. Normally, our stress builds and builds over time, but we don't notice it until it becomes a big problem. Muscle tension may build up in our bodies all day long, but we tend not to notice until it turns into a pounding headache.

Practice noticing how you are doing throughout the day. Of course, stress and muscle tension are uncomfortable, so you might not like what you notice. However, it is better to know what is happening so you can take action to prevent it from getting even worse.

To help you get started in becoming more aware of your stress, take some time to fill out the worksheet below. If you have trouble coming up with things, you might ask a trusted friend or family member what they have noticed in the past. The ones closest to us often notice that we are getting stressed before we do.

Before you look at the more subtle, early signs of stress, get in touch with what it's like when you're really stressed out. When you have hit the level of very high stress, what is it like for you? Each time may be a little different, but think back to the last couple of times you experienced high levels of stress.

What thoughts tend to come up in your mind when you are stressed out?

_____

_____

_____

What other emotions tend to come up when you are stressed out?

_____

_____

_____

What do you tend to feel in your body when you are stressed out? (tension in your back or shoulders, headaches, queasiness in your stomach, heart pounding, etc.)

_____

_____

_____

What do you tend to do when you get stressed out? (snap at others, pace, isolate yourself, etc.)

_____

_____

_____

Now, see if you can remember, or practice noticing, the very earliest signs that your stress levels are just beginning to rise. It will be much easier to do something to lower the stress when it is just starting.

What situations tend to trigger stress for you? (being around certain people, giving presentations, being asked to do certain things are work, etc.)

_____

_____

_____

What thoughts come into your mind when you are first starting to get stressed?

_____

_____

_____

What emotions start to come up when you are starting to get stressed?

_____

_____

_____

What are the earliest signs of stress in your body?

_____

_____

_____

What actions or behaviors do you do when you are first starting to get stressed?

_____

_____

_____

Making a Self-Care Action Plan

When you become better able to notice the signs that stress is building, you can pro-actively take steps to reduce it, or at least to prevent it from getting worse. When a situation causes us stress, it is easy to get caught up in what needs to be done about it, and to focus on taking care of the needs of others. Some people may even feel like self-care is selfish, or that they don't deserve to do good things for themselves.

While you may well need to take action when called for by a stressful situation, remember to keep asking yourself, "**What do I need to do to take care of myself as I'm dealing with this situation?**" You might be able to push yourself for a while (especially when you're young), but stress will catch up with you over time. You'll be no good to anybody if you don't take care of yourself.

Also, remember to build more self-care into your daily life. Don't wait until you get overwhelmed. While it is important to learn to respond to stress, regularly taking care of yourself makes you more resilient. You can think of your stress level as a water level. If you are standing in water that is up to your chin, every little wave that comes along will feel like it is going to drown you. However, if you can get the water level down to your waist or lower, it will take a much bigger wave to knock you off your feet. Likewise, if your stress is always high, almost everything will feel like a big deal. If you can get your overall stress level down, you'll be much better at rolling with the inevitable problems that life will throw at you.

Once you notice the signs that you are starting to get overwhelmed, it's good to have a plan to reduce your stress and get you in a better place. Since it can be really hard to think of proactive things to do when you are feeling stressed out, it is a good idea to write down your plan ahead of time, when you can think more clearly. You might be tempted to ignore the signs of rising stress, but make a promise to yourself to look over this action plan when you do notice those signs.

Let's start by bringing to mind the positive reasons you have to stay healthy. What are your values? Who and what are important to you?

_____

_____

_____

_____

Being kind to your own body helps bring down the stress response. Examples include taking a bubble bath, exercising, taking some deep breaths, indulging in a short afternoon nap, getting a massage, or practicing mindfulness.

What are some things you can do to be kind to your body (in moderation, of course)?

_____

_____

Too often, we get so caught up in earning a living and taking care of our household that we forget to make time for enjoyable activities. Think back on the things you used to do for fun, or explore some new activities that you think you might enjoy. When you first start doing them, you might feel like you are "wasting time," but this feeling will pass as you find more balance in your life. You might also feel like you don't enjoy them, but do them at least a few times before deciding if you really don't enjoy them or if that's just the stress talking.

What hobbies or activities do you do, or would like to try, to take care of yourself?

_____

_____

Getting small tasks accomplished can also reduce our stress. When there is too much to do, we feel overwhelmed, but breaking things down into small tasks helps us feel like we got something done and off our minds. If the whole house is a mess, just start by cleaning out one closet, or even just one drawer in your dresser. If you have to mow your lawn, you might not enjoy doing it, but you will feel good knowing it's done. Also, take some time to decide if something really needs to be done, or if you are putting unrealistic expectations on yourself.

What small things could you do to get them off your mind?

_____

_____

Social support can be a very important way to get through difficult times. Talking with friends, family, spiritual leaders, teachers, therapists, and even animals can help us get perspective on our problems, and remind us how important connection is.

Who can you call on for support when you start to get overwhelmed?

_____

_____

_____

_____

UNDERSTANDING ANXIETY

Anxiety is basically an ongoing sympathetic nervous system response. Anxiety disorders include phobias, generalized anxiety disorder, obsessive-compulsive disorder, health anxiety, obsessive-compulsive disorder, panic disorder, posttraumatic stress disorder, panic disorder, and eating disorders. We will also discuss special considerations for working with children and anxiety later in this chapter.

All anxiety disorders have in common a strong stress reaction, strong emotions and body sensations, and unrelenting thoughts. In a very real way, clients with anxiety are often "addicted" to their thinking, because while they are in the mental realm of thoughts, they are trying to avoid the discomfort of their body sensations. Direct exposure to bodily sensations, waiting for the sensations to rise and fall, will undermine the "fuel" for the compulsive thinking.

As with all clinical work, make sure the client is getting proper medical checkups to rule out issues like thyroid or glandular problems. Also, be sure to assess for substance intake, including stimulants like caffeine and energy drinks. Sometimes clients do not realize that drinking a 12-pack of Red Bull every day might just have an impact on their anxiety. It is also important to inquire about anxiolytics like Valium or Xanax. Benzodiazepines have been shown to interfere with exposure therapy (Rosen, Greenbaum, Schnurr, Holmes, Brennan, et al., 2013), because the individual cannot be as aware of body sensations during the exposure process. Clients on a steady dose of a benzodiazepines often have great difficulty withdrawing. Since they work immediately, clients are reluctant to stop taking them. Also, due to the "rebound effect," clients often experience even worse anxiety as they withdraw until their brain receptors can rebalance themselves. Even clients on milder forms, such as Klonopin, often report very uncomfortable withdrawal symptoms.

If clients are not on a steady dose, but only take something like Xanax occasionally, I will recommend (in consultation with their prescriber, of course) that the next time they really feel like they need to take it, to go ahead and take it. However, I suggest that they simply hold it in their hands and wait 10 seconds before they take it. Maybe the next time, they will be able to wait 20 seconds, or 30 seconds, 1 minute, 5 minutes, 10 minutes. Of course, in therapy, we are also working on helping them struggle less with anxiety, and on reducing their overall life stress levels, and eventually they find that the anxiety passes without the need to take the Xanax.

Because of the classical conditioning component, exposure therapy is the best way to treat anxiety disorders.

Tips for Working with Phobias and Generalized Anxiety

Phobias are a "simple" form of anxiety in the sense that they come about when the anxiety response becomes classically conditioned to a specific stimulus. Avoidance strategies, because they immediately lower the fear a little, become negatively reinforced.

I once had a client with a fear of snakes. She was hiking on a mountain trail, and stepped on what she thought was a big stick. It turned out to be a rattlesnake, and the client jumped with fear as the snake coiled up and shook its rattle.

Naturally, most human beings would be fearful in such a situation. For this client, the incident caused her so much anxiety that she worked hard to avoid anything related to snakes, and stopped going on outdoor walks. When she thought about walking on a trail, it created anxiety, so she would decide to avoid the walks, which dropped her anxiety a little. This negative reinforcement cycle of avoidance was beginning to cause problems for her, because her family wanted her to go on hikes with them.

Since this kind of fear and anxiety becomes classically conditioned in the stress response system, talking about the fears using the language centers of the cortex rarely does any good, and often serves to foster more avoidance. The best treatment to extinguish the classically conditioned fear and anxiety response is exposure therapy.

One can start with mild exposures and move up a hierarchy very gradually, as in systematic desensitization (which most clients prefer), or one can do a major exposure all at once, which is called flooding. Either way, the most important component is that clients face what triggers the fear, and do *absolutely nothing*. Clients with phobias never do nothing – when they feel the anxiety, they try to avoid it through such things as moving away, using a substance like alcohol, distracting themselves, or going off into the mental world of thinking. The crucial ingredient in exposure therapy is to allow the client to experience the anxiety, watch it rise with the extinction burst, and allow it to crest and fall. Even if the client starts out rating the fear as an 8 out of 10, then it rises to a 10 out of 10, and drops back down to a 9 out of 10, it is a success. Personally, I prefer to wait until it drops to at least a 7 out of 10, so the person ends up better off than when they started. However, the key is that they experience physically, not intellectually, that staying with it allows it to drop, since their fear is that the anxiety will go up forever. Cresting is key, not necessarily getting it down to 1 out of 10.

It is important to receive good training in doing exposure therapy. Before engaging clients in exposure work, be sure to build rapport so that they will trust you enough to face their fears. It is also important to provide the rationale for why feeling more uncomfortable in the short run will help in the long run.

Personally, I prefer to give clients just a small taste of the benefits of exposure therapy in the very first session, using a very mild stimulus (or their own body sensations), so they can experience that feeling it directly helps them break out of the cycle of struggle. Also, when doing exposure work, allow enough time in the session for the anxiety to come down at least a little. Since cresting is a crucial ingredient, do not start an exposure five minutes before the end of a therapy session. Using a heart rate variability monitor is another way of getting an objective measure for how distressed a client is feeling.

While clients with phobias exhibit fear of specific objects, those with generalized anxiety disorder (GAD) feel fear and anxiety about a number of different life situations. It can be difficult if not impossible to directly expose a client with GAD to everything they fear.

In a very real sense, the root of the problem with GAD is anxiety about feeling anxiety. A client may feel anxious about finances, so decides to avoid dealing with finances. The client may feel anxious about driving a car, so decides to avoid driving. Since being around people is anxiety-provoking, the client decides to avoid social situations. Over time, the client ends up living a very restricted life. When clients learn to feel the anxiety itself more directly, letting go of struggle and allowing it to naturally rise and fall, they begin to let go of their anxiety about the anxiety.

Because of their patterns of avoidance, individuals with GAD usually give up on important, meaningful things in their lives. The therapist can explore the costs of avoidance, and clarify what clients' values are. Since thoughts and feelings cannot control behavior, if clients are willing to have these even when they are uncomfortable, they can learn to take committed action to move toward a richer, more fulfilling life (Hayes, Strosahl, & Wilson, 2012).

The next worksheet can be a useful tool for clients to understand and work more wisely with anxiety.

Living with Anxiety

If you have been struggling with anxiety, you know how much impact it can have on your life every single day. Regardless of how it gets started, anxiety tends to create a vicious cycle in which the more you try to get rid of it, the worse it gets. You become more and more desperate to make it go away, and while there may be certain times it gets better, it somehow continues to rear its ugly head, and often at the worst and most inconvenient times.

There are many factors involved in creating and maintaining anxiety. Anxiety is simply a ramped up stress response, which your body is doing to try to help you deal with problems. However, it is meant to be a short-term response, so if it is lasting a while, it is important to find the underlying causes. Get a medical checkup, and pay attention to things like caffeine or energy drink intake. Try to get enough sleep, eat reasonably healthy meals, and make time in your daily life to relax. Regular exercise has been shown to significantly help with stress and mental health.

However, if you have tried these things, and anxiety is still interfering with your life, it is important to get professional help to break out of the anxiety trap.

Ironically, it is our very attempt to avoid anxiety that often keeps the cycle going. Of course, no rational human being wants to feel anxiety! We therefore try to avoid situations that might trigger it, attempt to distract ourselves from thinking about anxious things, and battle with the anxiety in the hopes that doing so will get rid of it. Unfortunately, our anxiety about feeling anxiety keeps it going.

Anxiety is just a messenger. There are times when anxiety gives you very important information, like telling you it would be a bad idea to walk out into oncoming traffic. When you listen to the messenger, it gives you information, then tends to subside. If you ignore or fight with the messenger, it keeps trying to deliver its message.

When you notice yourself thinking compulsively, it may be a sign that the real problem is that you are trying to avoid feeling the message of anxiety. One approach in this worksheet is the practice of moving your attention to your own body. As you'll experience below, this will let you receive the message, even though it might be uncomfortable. Whether or not it goes away, you can then choose what you want to do, instead of letting the anxiety and the thoughts make all your decisions for you.

Many people think that they will wait for the anxiety to go away before they live their lives, and then find themselves waiting for years. Can you remember a time when you wanted something so badly that you were willing to feel some anxiety in order to do it? It can be difficult, and definitely uncomfortable to feel anxiety, but the anxiety is more likely to lessen when you are living a fulfilling life.

The first step is to get in touch with the anxiety, explore the cost of avoidance, and clarify what is really important to you. Get started right now by taking some time to work through the questions following, and later discuss them with a professional.

Where in your body do you tend to feel your anxiety the most? Is it always in the same place, or does it float between multiple places? How does it change with time?

_____

_____

_____

What other emotions tend to accompany the anxiety? Do certain ones come up in specific situations? Where do you feel them in your body?

_____

_____

_____

What thoughts tend to arise when you are feeling anxious? Do the same thoughts keep coming up, or do they change rapidly? What are your "top 5" anxious thoughts?

_____

_____

_____

What situations, people, or things do you avoid? What important things, relationships, or activities have you given up in your life in your attempts to avoid feeling anxious?

_____

_____

_____

What would you like to do or have more of in your life? What would make your life more meaningful? Can you rediscover the things that are so important that you would be willing to experience some anxiety in order to live a more fulfilling life?

_____

_____

_____

What concrete thing can you do today, however small, to face some of the anxiety and do something that matters to you? What small steps can you take in the coming week, month, and year?

_____

_____

_____

OBSESSIVE-COMPULSIVE DISORDER

Obsessive-compulsive disorder (OCD) is characterized by persistent obsessions and/or behavioral compulsions. People who suffer from OCD know intellectually that their obsessions or compulsions are not logical, but they feel trapped in a cycle, because they cannot stand the feelings of anxiety. The thoughts or behaviors provide at least momentary relief, and provide distraction from the anxiety sensations in the body. The view of OCD as an attempt to avoid feelings is confirmed by the fact that the symptoms tend to worsen in times of stress.

Anyone can become obsessed with thoughts. Trying not to think of something is a sure-fire way to keep it in your mind, as when someone asks you to try not to think of a green elephant. When there is underlying anxiety, clients can get stuck in the mental realm of thinking to avoid feeling the unpleasant anxiety sensations in their bodies.

I once attended an excellent workshop with a psychologist named Patrick McGrath on Exposure and Response Prevention (2007; 2013). Dr. McGrath (2013) shared a story about a woman who had to take a subway to get to her college classes. At the platform station where she waited, the trains rushed by at high speeds. There were no railings, and the tracks were several feet below the platform. As she was standing there, she had a random thought about pushing someone off the platform down onto the tracks when a train went by. She was very surprised to have had such a thought, and became very anxious. She could not stand the anxiety of having such a thought, and left the train station. After a month or so of missing classes, she finally decided to seek professional help.

Dr. McGrath of course conducted a thorough intake, ruling out such things as psychosis, trauma, and antisocial personality disorder (you will soon see why this was important). At one point, Dr. McGrath said, "You know, there is a platform station like that very near here. Would you be willing to go there with me?" Perhaps because of the rapport they developed, or maybe out of sheer desperation, she agreed to go.

When they got there, Dr. McGrath walked right up to the edge of the platform, where he could clearly see the tracks below, and could feel the breeze of the passing trains as they whipped past. He asked the client to stand directly behind him and to place her hand on his shoulder. He then looked back at her and said, "When the next train comes by, I want you to push me as hard as you can!"

Of course, since Dr. McGrath was able to tell the story, he was not killed. After a number of trains went by, he faced the client and asked, "You're not *really* going to push me in front of a train, are you?" The young woman smiled and shook her head. "You had a *thought* about pushing someone in front of a train," he continued. "A thought cannot force you to do anything." After directly facing her distressing thoughts and her anxiety, the woman was able to go back to school.

Decentering, or defusion, which involves the recognition that internal experiences like thoughts and emotions cannot control behavior, is very important for clients. They can choose to do what is important to them even if unpleasant thoughts and feelings are still there.

Tips for Using Imaginal Exposure

Employing imaginal exposure can be helpful when you are restricted to being in an office setting. I once had a client who was very anxious about driving, and it was greatly impacting her life as a parent who needed to take her kids to important places. While she said she knew it was ridiculous, she could not stop worrying about running over somebody. When she felt a bump, she could not get rid of the thought that it could have been a person, which made her very anxious. She would then turn around and drive past the place she thought she felt the bump and check, and seeing that no one had been run over, her anxiety would go down a little (negative reinforcement of the checking behavior). But because she still had a little anxiety, she would then have a thought that maybe she did not look hard enough, which sparked more anxiety, which made her want to check again.

After getting to know this client, I decided that imaginal exposure would be helpful. I realized that a big part of her anxiety about driving was the thought of running someone over, so I talked with her about moving directly into this. She was willing, so I connected her to the HRV monitor. I asked her to close her eyes, and to imagine herself walking out to her car in as much detail as possible, using all of her senses.

Different clients respond differently to imaginal exposure. Some clients can clearly visualize scenes in their minds, some need "over-the-top" stimulation, and some do not respond very well at all. Since this client was not feeling very anxious imagining being in her car, I asked her to imagine driving around. This, too, did not evoke much anxiety. Realizing that her biggest fear was running over someone, I decided to have her imagine a man walking out in front of her car. I noticed a definite rise in the HRV monitor, but it was not overly high, so I continued to paint a clear picture of her hitting the man. She imagined hitting his knees with the bumper, watching him bounce on the hood, and seeing his face pressed against the windshield. She stayed with the images until the anxiety came down.

While I would not conduct such a visualization with a client with antisocial personality disorder, in this case, the exposure was very helpful. Since the client was no longer afraid of thinking about running over someone, she was able to let go of thinking about not thinking about it.

Since strong thoughts are often a significant component of OCD, as well as other anxiety disorders, the following worksheet gives suggestions for working with them more wisely.

When Strong Thoughts
Just Won't Go Away

Sometimes, despite our best efforts, we just can't get strong distressing thoughts out of our heads. When we have real problems in our lives, it can be very useful to think about what we need to do about them. But when the thoughts seem to keep spiraling, our stress goes up, and we become less able to think clearly.

At times, you might be able to tell yourself not to worry, that things will be all right. There may be times when you are able to plant a positive thought in your mind to shift your thinking. But when you notice that trying to replace your thoughts is not working, and is only fueling more arguments with yourself inside your head, there are some different options for breaking out of that vicious circle.

The first step is to look directly at what the thoughts are, so you are clear about what you're dealing with.

What are the strong distressful thoughts in your mind right now? Are they new, or do they get stuck in your head often?

_____

_____

_____

_____

_____

_____

When these thoughts are in your head, what emotions come along with them?

_____

_____

_____

_____

_____

_____

What do you notice in your body when these thoughts are in your head? (For example, fast heartbeat, tense muscles, queasy feeling in your stomach, etc.)

_____

_____

_____

_____

_____

_____

The strong thoughts may be about something very important that you have to deal with in your life, but when they overwhelm you, your first priority needs to be taking care of yourself. After all, when you are in a calmer place, you will be better able to handle what's going on. What self-care things can you do for yourself? (for example, take a walk, relax in a hot bath, take some deep breaths, look outside at the trees, etc.)

_____

_____

_____

_____

_____

_____

Your thoughts probably feel very real to you when they are strong, but remember that they are only sounds inside your head. You are having thoughts, but they are not you. Thoughts might tell you what to do, but it's up to you to decide what you want to do in each moment. You can watch the thoughts come and go instead of arguing with them. You can write down your thoughts in a journal, or talk to a friend or therapist, to get them out of your head and to get perspective on them. As funny as it sounds, you can also repeat strong thoughts over and over and over again – say them out loud for at least 30 seconds, and they will tend to lose some of their emotional punch.

It may also be helpful to remember that the more you fight your thoughts, the stronger they tend to become. After all, you are arguing with yourself, so how can you win against yourself? It takes practice, but instead of trying to control them, you can learn to let the thoughts do whatever they want to do. You can just go ahead and do what is important to you to do in your life, whatever the thoughts try to tell you.

HEALTH ANXIETY

Health anxiety, formerly known as hypochondriasis, is an anxiety disorder in which clients ruminate or worry about their bodies and their health. At some level, they know their anxiety is excessive, but it tends to be kept alive by the very real possibility that something could go wrong with their health, even if there is only a remote chance.

Clients often find it helpful when I reframe their sensitivity to their own bodies as a gift, since many people are completely unaware of the workings of their physical organism. The problem lies in the strong thoughts and emotions that have become associated with what they notice in their bodies. Though I would not necessarily say this to clients, if they claim to be feeling their bodies too much, I will actually help them feel their bodies more directly, which undercuts the distraction of ruminative thoughts.

Distraction can work, but only temporarily, and it takes a lot of energy. Also, you would not want to teach someone with medical issues to always use distraction, since catching a medical issue early enough can prevent more serious problems in the future.

I once had a client who had survived a very serious heart attack. The surgery was intense, and he still felt the scar and discomfort in his chest. He had gone back to work, but felt very drained by the end of the day. He was struggling with anxiety, and reported being "hyperaware" of his chest.

I asked the client if he would be willing to try an experiment with me, and he agreed. I asked him to rate his currently level of anxiety on a scale of 1 to 10, and he replied that it was a 7. When I asked him to pinpoint the source of the anxiety, he quickly identified that it was in his chest. "This may sound strange," I said, "but I'd like you to keep your awareness on the sensations in your chest. Explore them like a scientist, investigating the physical sensations you notice there. The anxiety is likely to go up some at first, and your thoughts will probably jump all over the place, remembering the heart attack and the surgery, or worrying about how you will get your work done in the future. Just notice when your attention goes off with the thoughts, and keep gently bringing your awareness back to the chest. Get in touch with the sensations, and notice if they are sharp or dull, waxing or waning, staying in the same place or moving around."

In only a few minutes, the client was amazed that his anxiety dropped to a 3 out of 10. By staying with the underlying sensations, he experienced an "extinction burst" at first, but then the anxiety dropped, because he was no longer avoiding the sensations by getting caught up in thinking.

The following worksheet may be helpful for clients to better understand health anxiety.

Living with Health Anxiety

Everyone worries about their health sometimes, but when the worry becomes excessive, and interferes with your enjoyment of life, you may be diagnosed with health anxiety disorder. The anxiety can become all-consuming, and the harder you try not to worry about your body, the worse it seems to get.

People may tell you not to worry about it, but you can't just ignore your body. Noticing a medical issue early enough could save your life! Your friends probably don't understand, and may wonder why you can't just stop worrying. Yet, in your mind, you know that bad things really do happen to bodies. You see it in the news all the time. You know people get cancer. You have definitely had real health problems in your past. Maybe friends or relatives have actually died from health problems – none of that is just "in your head"!

Sensitivity, or awareness of your own body, is actually a gift! Many people ignore what their bodies tell them, and it gets them into trouble. Noticing is not the problem. The real problem is what happens after you notice something about your body, or after you think of something that could go wrong. Your thoughts carry you away to all kinds of "what-if" scenarios, which sparks anxiety, which sparks more worrisome thoughts, which sparks more anxiety.

You have probably tried distracting yourself to get a break from the anxiety, but I'll bet it's hard to keep that up constantly. Distraction can take a lot of time and energy, and could even keep you from catching real health problems if they do arise.

For example, a breast cancer survivor might suddenly notice a bump on her chest, and immediately be flooded with anxiety. "Oh no! Not a recurrence! I never finished writing my will! I'm too young to die! I really wanted see my daughter get married! She'll be so sad to have a wedding without me!"

While such thoughts and feelings are natural, they tend to carry us away and keep the anxiety going. We can learn to remind ourselves to come back to the moment, and make a clear decision. For the person who found that bump, the only reality she knows in that moment is that she feels a bump, and that there is of course some anxiety rising up. She can then make a more conscious decision about what to do. If she is in the middle of an important meeting, she may decide to address it a little later. She may decide to call the doctor for an opinion. She may decide to wait until her next doctor appointment if it is coming up soon. She may even notice that the bump is exactly the same on both sides of her chest, and that perhaps she was only feeling a rib. Whatever it turns out to be, by coming back to what she really knows in the present moment, she can begin to interrupt the old patterns of automatic worrying that would have carried her off all day long in the past.

This is simple, but not always easy to do. You may have a lifelong history of worrying, so be patient with yourself as you learn to relate differently to your body and your anxiety.

As you have likely noticed, when your overall life stress or anxiety is high, your health anxiety tends to be worse. Be sure to make time to take care of yourself on a regular basis to help prevent some of the anxiety peaks.

If your anxiety has been intense, you may have given up on the things that were important to you. When you are living a fulfilling life, whatever that means to you, you will probably get less caught up in all the anxiety.

Use the worksheet to practice relating differently to your thoughts, emotions, and body sensations. Fill it out when you are calm as well as when you are anxious, and see if you notice any patterns.

What are you noticing in your body right now? Be as specific as you can. Do the sensations change with time? In what way?

_____

_____

_____

What emotions are you feeling? How intense are they? Do they change with time? If so, how?

_____

_____

_____

What thoughts are popping up in your mind right now? Are these new thoughts, or old familiar ones? How strong and real do they seem to you? Do you believe all of them, or are they old recordings being played back in your mind?

_____

_____

_____

What do you typically do when you begin worrying about your health? What behaviors do you tend to do? What do you tend to avoid?

_____

_____

_____

How has your health anxiety been useful to you in the past? In what ways has it been a good thing?

_____

_____

_____

In what ways has your health anxiety created problems for you? What has been the cost of the worrying to yourself and those around you? What important things have you given up in your struggles with the anxiety?

_____

_____

_____

What do you value in life? What would make your life more meaningful? Are you willing to feel some of the anxiety in order to live a more fulfilling life?

_____

_____

_____

What healthy things can you do to take care of yourself, both right now and in the long-term? What self-care activities help bring your stress down? Who can you count on for support?

_____

_____

_____

✀

Above all, remember to be kind to yourself when things get difficult. After all, they are your own thoughts, your own feelings, and your own body sensations. They deserve compassion, just as you do.

PANIC DISORDER

Panic attacks are intense episodes of anxiety that can be very frightening for clients, as well as for untrained therapists. As with other forms of anxiety, be sure to do a thorough clinical intake to look for underlying or comorbid diagnoses like PTSD or substance use disorder. Make sure clients have received competent medical assessments, and ask them about the frequency and quantity of stimulant intake, such as caffeine, energy drinks, or Adderall. Also, individuals with panic disorder often breathe shallowly from the chest, so teaching them diaphragmatic breathing can be quite helpful (see the Breathing and Stress handout in the stress section).

It is important for clients to recognize that their overall life stress level will have a major impact on the frequency of panic attacks, so be sure to address long-term self-care with clients. However, until their life stress becomes more manageable, clients will need concrete tools for what to do during a panic attack.

I once had a young man come to me with a lifetime history of anxiety. I asked him the "magic wand" question -- "If all your anxiety were suddenly gone, what would your life be like?" He responded by saying, "I have no idea. I've been anxious my whole life. I can't even imagine what it would be like to not have any anxiety."

In fact, right in front of me, in the very first session, a full-blown panic attack came on. Since he had already informed me that he was having frequent panic attacks, and that he had been getting medical checkups, I knew it was not a medical emergency, though I reassured him that I had received EMT training and could call 911 if necessary.

Most people instinctively fight their own panic attacks, since they are so terrifying, so I invited him to practice staying with it, in a kind of exposure therapy. "I know this is very scary, and you've had a lot of these before, but if you're willing, let's try something different. As best you can, let go of struggling with what is happening, and see if you can describe it to me as it unfolds. Like a scientist describing a phenomenon, or a sports announcer giving the blow-by-blow, tell me what you are experiencing, especially in your physical body."

The first thing he said was, "I feel like I'm going to throw up!" Of course, I moved the trash can in front of him just in case, though he later told me he had not thrown up in years.

I used my own ability to stay present to model an attitude of letting go of some of the struggle. "I know this is very difficult, but can you tell me what else you are noticing, especially in your body?"

He quickly replied, "I feel like I'm going to die!" Many people have this thought during a panic attack, because they are experiencing very intense, strong, physiological sensations. The stress response kicks into overdrive to prepare for a life and death struggle, triggering normally helpful responses like fast heart rate, increased blood pressure, and shallow breathing.

"Okay, so you noticed a thought that you feel like you're going to die, and I'm sure it is really uncomfortable. I know this is hard right now, but can you describe what you are feeling physically in your body?" Since he was feeling overwhelmed at that moment, it would not have been helpful to talk about exposure therapy and how thoughts can be a distraction, so I was providing external guidance back into the experience.

"Well, I feel a queasiness in my stomach, and I'm concerned that I'm getting nauseous, and I'm afraid I might throw up, and that would be embarrassing, and I don't want to ruin your nice carpet..."

"So you noticed queasiness in your stomach, then you starting thinking about my carpet. What else are you experiencing, especially in your body?" In effect, I was using my words as a scaffolding for the client's attention. Naturally, no one wants to feel panic, so he struggled with it and tried to think of other things. I was helping to guide his attention back to the underlying body sensations to facilitate exposure.

Of course, the client did not jump up at the end of the panic attack and say, "Thanks Doc, I'm cured!" However, he learned that he could feel the sensations more directly and not explode. Since panic attacks and anxiety are so uncomfortable, that is the last thing most clients would think to do. Ironically, the more we fight with anxiety, the more we prolong it. Anticipatory anxiety, or the anxiety about having anxiety, tends to make it more likely for a panic attack to happen. By learning to move into it, and learning to be more comfortable with the discomfort, it is more likely to pass.

The following handout can help clients make sense of panic, and gives them some concrete suggestions for what to do when a panic attack comes on.

Surviving Panic Attacks

If you suffer from panic attacks, you know how terrifying they can be. What you are experiencing is not "all in your head." The physical responses are very real. Your heart pounds, your blood pressure shoots up, your head spins, and your mind races. It feels as if you are going to die.

Though it may feel like you are going to, no one has ever exploded from a panic attack. Your body is doing something that would normally save your life. When you perceive a threat, your stress response system kicks up to prepare you to fight, flee, or freeze until the danger has passed.

A panic attack is the stress response system kicking into high gear. When there is not a physical threat in front of us, people usually try to suppress this response. Ironically, the more you fight panic, the worse it gets. **Rather than fighting the waves of panic, try to surf the waves. Remember that no storm lasts forever, and as unpleasant as it might get at times, these storms will pass too.**

Between panic attacks, do your best to take care of yourself. Lowering your overall levels of stress will help to prevent full-blown panic attacks from coming back. Though you can learn to ride out the panic, the good news is that learning how to reduce your life stress will prevent them in the first place.

Here are some things to do when you feel a panic attack coming on:

OBSERVE WHAT IS HAPPENING
Because panic attacks are so frightening, your first urge will probably be to distract yourself. As scary as it seems, since it's already happening anyway, just stay with it as best you can. Notice what is happening, like a scientist observing some interesting phenomenon, or like a sports announcer giving a blow-by-blow report.

LET GO OF RESISTANCE
The feelings that come up are so unpleasant that you will want to fight them. Getting anxious about your anxiety only makes it worse. It's your own body – try not to fight with it.

BE KIND TO YOURSELF
Sometimes we get upset with ourselves for having so much anxiety, or berate ourselves for not getting better fast enough. Remind yourself that you are doing the best you can.

FEEL YOUR BODY MORE DIRECTLY
All the racing thoughts you are having are your brain's attempt to get your mind off the scary feelings in your body. However, if you can feel your body more directly, they will get a little worse at first, but will usually pass more quickly. Place your hands on your heart, your stomach, or wherever you feel the anxiety most strongly. Cradle your emotions as if they were a crying baby. Screaming at a crying baby only makes things worse - the best way to soothe a baby, or your emotions, is to be kind and gentle with them.

BREATHE AS DEEPLY AS YOU CAN FROM YOUR STOMACH

You will likely notice that you are breathing quickly from your chest. Do your best to breathe more deeply and slowly from your belly - this stimulates the vagus nerve to trigger your body's relaxation response. It will probably feel weird at first, or make you feel light-headed for a little while, but stay with it.

WAIT FOR IT TO PASS

No storm lasts forever. Ironically, the more you want it to be over, the more anxiety you create, and the more likely it is to linger on. Just watch as patiently as you can for the point where the anxiety crests and begins to subside.

Read over these principles again and again, even if you don't believe them right away. Cut this summary out and keep it in your purse or wallet:

When Panic Arises

- Observe what is happening
- Let go of resistance
- Be kind to yourself
- Feel your body more directly
- Breathe as deeply as you can from your stomach
- Wait for it to pass

TRAUMA

As a mental health professional, no matter what type of service you provide or population you serve, it is important to receive training in recognizing and working with trauma survivors. In a world full of violence, posttraumatic stress disorder (PTSD) is sadly a very common presenting issue, or may be something that comes up later after working through other initial issues. Individuals with PTSD can present with symptoms of stress, anxiety, depression, bipolar disorder, dissociation, borderline personality disorder, neurocognitive disorders, substance use disorder, attention deficit/hyperactivity disorder, and/or oppositional defiant disorder, so it is important to be able to make a differential diagnosis.

By definition, an individual with PTSD experienced or witnessed something that was extremely frightening, even life-threatening. The limbic system therefore puts a strong emotional charge on the memories so that the person does not forget it, since it will be important to learn from the experiences for future survival. Yet, the conscious thinking mind, or cortex, naturally wants to forget the horrific memory. The ensuing battle results in the emotions bursting out in re-experiencing symptoms, such as flashbacks and nightmares. Though it rarely happens in the therapy room, if someone begins having flashbacks or dissociation experiences, it is important for the therapist to remain calm. Asking them questions about where they are and what they see and hear around them can help to engage the frontal lobes to ground them in the present moment.

Dissociation is common for individuals with PTSD. It is important to understand that at the time of the trauma, especially if it was ongoing, dissociation was likely a useful defense mechanism used by the brain to avoid feeling the terrible emotions and body sensations that were going on. Rather than take away a trauma survivor's defense mechanisms, we can begin to give them new tools for staying present with the difficult thoughts, emotions, and feelings in their bodies.

It is crucial to receive competent training to work with trauma survivors, as an untrained clinician can create more harm for these clients. For example, solely emphasizing the graphic details of past traumas is very uncomfortable for most clients, and in fact, may only serve to re-traumatize them. After all, by definition, a person with PTSD experienced something very threatening, so any human being would react strongly to it. It is much more important to process distressing emotions, especially as they intrude into and interfere with the client's daily functioning.

In the evidence-based treatment known as Cognitive Processing Therapy (CPT: Chard, 2005; Resick, Galovski, Uhlmansiek, Scher, Clum, et al., 2008), one of the emphases is on working with "stuck points," or problematic beliefs that interfere with recovery (e.g., "It is my fault my friend died. I should have seen the attack coming. I should never have left my house. I should be dead, not my friend.").

Another evidence-based intervention for PTSD is Prolonged Exposure (PE: Foa, Hembree, & Rothbaum, 2007). PE operates on the well-researched science of classical and operant conditioning, utilizing extinction through exposure therapy. A hierarchy of feared or avoided situations is created, and after learning relaxation techniques such as deep breathing, clients practice moving through imaginal and in vivo feared situations. While the research shows that PE clearly works, many clients express great discomfort in undergoing this treatment, or will not even attempt to go through it.

Interestingly, an intervention known as Present-Centered Therapy (PCT: Frost, Laska, & Wampold, 2014; Schnurr, Friedman, Engel, Foa, Shea, et al., 2007) has also been shown to be helpful in the treatment of PTSD. Originally created to operate as a control group in PTSD research, it was found to be as effective as other treatments in three out of five studies, and is superior to wait-list control conditions with very large effect sizes for the symptoms of PTSD (Frost, Laska, & Wampold, 2014). PCT uses general clinical skills like genuineness, compassion, congruence, respect, and problem-solving skills rather than directly addressing past traumatic events. For this reason, PCT has a much lower dropout rate than other PTSD interventions, and can more easily be used by clinicians who do not have more in-depth training in CPT or PE.

When properly utilized, mindfulness appears to be a helpful adjunct to treating individuals with trauma. Mindfulness trains clients' attentional capacity to better notice and work with their own thoughts, helps them manage the strong emotions that come up, and can help ground them in the present moment.

PTSD symptoms can have a strong negative impact on a person's interpersonal relationships. Given that mindfulness can be helpful for relationships (Carson, Carson, Gil, & Baucom, 2004; Harris, 2009; Walser & Westrup, 2009) as well as in the treatment of PTSD, it has been added to the manualized, evidence-based intervention known as Cognitive-Behavioral Conjoint Therapy (CBCT: Monson & Fredman, 2012). Mindfulness-based cognitive-behavioral conjoint therapy for posttraumatic stress disorder (MB-CBCT: Luedtke, Davis, & Monson, 2015) teaches CBT principles and mindfulness skills to individuals with PTSD and their intimate partners to help them understand and heal from trauma while improving their relationships. The program consists of clients and their partners attending a weekend couples' retreat, followed by nine couples' sessions.

Even the most experienced clinicians among us can be significantly affected by the horrendous stories we hear. As therapists, we are susceptible to vicarious trauma, so it is very important to take care of ourselves when working with clients who have experienced serious trauma. Having our own personal mindfulness practice helps us stay present with clients and their strong emotions, which models for them that they can do it too. Developing our mindfulness skills also helps us process our own emotions and re-center ourselves after a difficult session.

The following worksheet can help clients better understand PTSD.

Understanding
Posttraumatic Stress Disorder (PTSD)

If you have been diagnosed with posttraumatic stress disorder, or PTSD, you have experienced or witnessed at least one life-threatening or very traumatic event, and you are still being affected by it.

Of course, anyone who goes through extreme events will be affected by them. Understanding PTSD may help you realize that what you are experiencing is a normal reaction to something extreme. Despite what you might think sometimes, you are not crazy.

If you have PTSD, you experienced something so horrifying that you do not want to think about it or remember it. Yet, your emotions are firing up strongly, because part of you knows that what you went through was so serious that remembering it could help save your life in the future. There is a battle going on between your cortex, which is the thinking part of your brain, and the limbic system, which is the emotional part of your brain.

This battle between thoughts and feelings takes a lot of energy, and sometimes the emotions burst out as "re-experiencing symptoms." You might have very vivid and emotional nightmares. The intense feelings of terror you felt in the past might get triggered by things that remind you of the trauma, sometimes without you even knowing why. Sometimes the memories will fire so strongly that you feel like you are back in the old trauma again. Known as "flashbacks," they can be very scary, and seem quite real. It may be helpful for you to know that these re-experiencing symptoms are just your own brain firing old emotional signals. Your brain is trying to protect you by getting you ready for danger, even though the danger may no longer exist. **When you notice re-experiencing symptoms coming up, practice grounding yourself in the present moment, to get your brain out of the past.** What do you see, hear, smell, taste, or feel right now, in this moment? If you fill your awareness with what is happening now, there will be less room in your brain for the old thoughts and memories, and the intense emotions will eventually pass.

Because these symptoms are so intense, people with PTSD work hard to avoid triggering them, and also struggle not to feel them. Avoidance only works temporarily, and if the triggers are never dealt with, the symptoms will continue, and the cycle of avoidance will go on and on.

Experiencing a serious trauma changes the way you view the world. Little things may not seem to matter much anymore, and your innocence about the world is shattered because you know how bad things can get. You become hypervigilant, because your brain is constantly worrying about where danger might come from next. You may be irritable and startle easily, because your stress system is amped up and ready to run, freeze, or fight. It is hard to trust people, and you may feel detached from others, so relationships become more difficult and chaotic. Negative thoughts may fill your brain, and it may be difficult to concentrate.

What happened to you was a terrible tragedy, and no one would blame you for getting stuck in those awful memories. But when you are stuck in the past, or constantly worried about the future, you stop living in this moment. There are now proven therapies for dealing with past traumas, if you are willing to go through the discomfort of the process. The major question is, are you willing to build a life worth living from this moment forward, even if you do still hurt, and even if you will still sometimes be affected by the past?

It can be very challenging to work through PTSD on your own. Working with a professional who has specific trauma-related expertise can help you navigate the ups and downs that inevitably arise when you are in the process of recovering your life. It is normal for things to get a little worse before they get better, so hang in there.

Work through the questions below with your therapist. Be patient with and kind to yourself if these questions bring up unpleasant feelings. If the feelings get too strong, take a break and come back to them later, or wait and go through them with your therapist.

What has the PTSD and the avoidance cost you? What damage has it done to you? What symptoms do you have? How has PTSD affected your life?

_____

_____

_____

_____

_____

What triggers your symptoms? What things, people, places, or situations do you avoid?

_____

_____

_____

_____

What kinds of thoughts and images pop up when you are getting distressed?

_____

_____

_____

_____

What emotions arise? How strong are they? How long do they usually last?

_____

_____

_____

What do you notice happening in your body when you are feeling distressed? Are those body feelings always there at some level, or only when things get bad? Do they change with time? If so, how?

_____

_____

_____

PTSD puts people in a survival mode, so it can be hard to think about living, and even more difficult to imagine thriving. You might have a hard time even imagining tomorrow, much less five or ten years from now, but having a direction for your life can help you regain a sense of meaning. What do you value?

What is important to you? Your brain may have trouble coming up with anything, so come back to this question over the next few days or weeks.

_____

_____

What short-term goals will help you move in the direction of what you value? What steps can you take to move forward? Even if some of the goals seem unachievable to your mind right now, what small step can you take to get started?

_____

_____

_____

Filing out this worksheet might bring up some old feelings. What can you do to take care of yourself right now? What activities can help calm you down? Do you have someone (human or animal) in your life who can give you support?

_____

_____

_____

❧

Remember to be kind to yourself during the recovery process. It is not a race – you can move at your own pace. If it feels like you are moving too fast, talk about it openly with your therapist.

EATING DISORDERS

In our modern society, which places high value on external appearances, eating disorders are alarmingly common. Almost everyone has some issues or anxieties around eating, and for some people, it becomes a significant disorder that interferes with their lives.

Although true for all mental health disorders, it is especially crucial to have proper training to work with eating disorders. It is estimated that the mortality rate for individuals with anorexia nervosa is 5% per decade (American Psychiatric Association, 2012). In their minds, individuals with anorexia nervosa may literally not see themselves as thin, similar to body dysmorphic disorder. As they become increasingly emaciated, they begin to show the physical symptoms of starvation, such as amenorrhea, hypotension, hypothermia, and bradycardia.

Overeating is also a common issue. Diets tend not to work for many people, because it sets up a cycle of struggle with food. Because eating feels good, people crave food to lower their anxiety or other unpleasant emotions, but after eating, they feel guilty, which sets up a vicious cycle. Instead of battling with themselves, it is important to help clients relate differently to food, and to help them better manage their cravings and their emotions (Albers, 2003).

In the MBSR, MBCT, and MBRP protocols, the first mindfulness exercise is to eat one raisin. Even though eating is not a focus of these programs, clients will often report that they ended up losing a few pounds that they had been meaning to lose without much effort. This is probably because they have learned to do things less automatically, and to savor their experiences. They also learn to feel and flow with their own emotions better, so probably use food less often as a means to distract themselves from their feelings. Working directly with the underlying ability to stay with one's own thoughts and emotions can be an important part of treatment.

There is now a nine-week program designed specifically for overeating called Mindfulness-Based Eating Awareness Training (MB-EAT), and the research thus far looks very promising (Kristeller & Bowman, 2015; Kristeller & Wolever, 2011). Some of the concepts from this program are presented in the next client worksheet.

Mindful Eating

Many people today have a love/hate relationship with food. You may feel like, "I can't live with it, and I can't live without it." Because of this, you may have fallen victim to a diet fad or two, promising to make you thin, happy, and attractive. While it is important to eat a healthy, balanced variety of foods, extreme diets rarely work. Even if you manage to lose a lot of weight through sheer willpower, it very often comes back again. The sense of deprivation tends to increase your cravings.

Emotions can become intimately connected with eating. After all, eating can be very pleasurable, and can provide a nice distraction from the stress and emotions in our daily lives. While food should be enjoyed, it does not work very well as an emotion regulation system. While it is fine to sometimes enjoy comfort food, if you develop the habit of using food to escape from unpleasant feelings, those feelings are usually still there when you are done eating. You may even add guilt and shame on top of them after eating too much, leading to a vicious cycle from which it is hard to break away.

Likewise, thoughts about food can be a distraction from the stress of daily life, and the thoughts can trigger cravings. Overeating can then trigger thoughts about being a "bad person" who "lacks control," or you may berate yourself if you do not look quite like the professional models on television. The voices and judgments of unkind friends or relatives may still be echoing through your head from many years ago. It is easy to get trapped in a vicious cycle of negative thoughts and overeating.

Eating mindfully is not about deprivation, but about changing our relationship with food. In other words, we can learn to break our emotional love/hate reactions to eating. Slow down a little and actually enjoy the taste of your food. Cut down on your distractions so you can really notice what you are eating. If you shovel your food down while watching TV, you will miss the flavor, and end up eating a lot more than you intended.

It might also be useful to know about a concept called "taste specific satiety." Basically, it means that your taste buds will acclimate to whatever tastes are in your mouth. All of our senses do this. If there is a bad smell in the room, and it isn't changing, you will cease to notice it after a while. For taste, 80% percent of the flavor of your food comes from the first three bites. Try it out for yourself the next time you eat. The first bite is usually bursting with flavor, but after the third bite, you're only getting 20% of the flavor. This can contribute to eating too much, because we try to chase after that flavor that we got from the first bite.

Another factor in overeating is that even though you may already be full, it takes about 15 minutes for your stomach to send the "I've had enough" signal to your brain. If you eat quickly, you can stuff yourself with a lot more food in those 15 minutes, which leads to a really uncomfortable, bloated feeling after you finally stop eating.

To make your eating more conscious and less automatic, briefly pause before you eat something and ask yourself the following two questions:

On a scale of 1-10, how hungry do I feel right now?

On a scale of 1-10, how full do I feel right now?

It might surprise you to discover that those numbers are often not related. You might feel full but also hungry. Or you might not feel full at all and yet not feel hungry at all. Whatever your numbers tend to be, watch the patterns. You are free to go ahead and eat whenever you choose, but by asking yourself these questions first, you will begin to cut back on automatic eating.

The environment is also important. Don't keep lots of junk food around the house. Doing so can make it far too easy to fall into automatic eating. Also, eat the healthier food first. In a study of lunch lines in schools, if the fruit was placed at the beginning of the line, kids took it, and then decided not to eat as much junk food. If they piled up their plates first with unhealthy foods, they were less likely to pick up and eat fruit if it was at the end of the lunch line.

Even the size of your plate has been shown to contribute to overeating. If you use a large plate, your brain wants to fill it full of food. If you use a smaller plate, you will tend to eat less.

Remember to make any changes to your eating patterns gradually. Drastic changes are difficult to maintain, and can put you on a roller coaster ride with your weight. Even cutting back 50-100 calories a day can result in losing 5-10 pounds per year.

Exercise, or some type of regular physical activity, is also important for health. Not only will it burn calories, it will give you more energy and vitality. Exercise has also been shown to improve mood and brain functioning, and to reduce stress and anxiety.

To get started on a path toward balanced eating, the worksheet below can help you better understand some of the automatic eating patterns that you might get stuck in.

What are the triggers in the environment that put you at risk for unhealthy eating? (For example, other people around you eating that way, others pushing you to eat more, too much food easily accessible, etc.)

_____

_____

_____

_____

What are the eating patterns that get you into trouble? What is it that you would like to change?

_____

_____

_____

What thoughts tend to come up in your mind before, after, and while you are eating? What self-judgments do you notice?

_____

_____

_____

_____

What emotions tend to come up for you before, after, and while you are eating?

_____

_____

_____

_____

What body sensations do you notice before, after, and while you are eating?

_____

_____

_____

When strong thoughts and emotions come up, what else can you do to take care of yourself, besides eating?

_____

_____

_____

Why do you want to change your eating habits? What are the bigger picture reasons for making these changes (to be more active, feel more alive, do more things with family, etc.)? Are you willing to sometimes have unpleasant thoughts and feelings for your big picture values?

_____

_____

_____

_____

_____

_____

_____

CHILDREN AND ANXIETY

Anxiety is becoming increasingly common in children today. A recent study by the American Psychological Association (2014) showed that the stress levels of teens are now as high as those of adults. Increased expectations for school performance, chores, and after-school sports and activities keep the stress response going. Fewer children have unstructured outdoor play because of these time demands and the constant distraction of electronic devices.

All this busyness and anxiety can also interfere with sleep. The National Sleep Foundation (2016) recommends that school-age children receive 9-11 hours of sleep a night, and that teenagers get 8-10 hours per night. However, many children go with much less, and end up with increased stress and decreased concentration.

Anxiety often manifests itself differently in children than in adults. Many children will complain about somatic symptoms, such as nausea and headaches. They may also express their anxiety through worrying about all types of unlikely future scenarios.

Since mindfulness is about being more present in the moment, people often ask me about teaching mindfulness to young children. I usually tell them that it is more likely that kids can teach us a thing or two about mindfulness. Children are naturally in the moment when they are young. However, as they grow up, they learn all kinds of ideas and thoughts, which can begin to obscure their natural state.

Randye Semple and Jennifer Lee (2011) have developed a curriculum for kids known as Mindfulness-Based Cognitive Therapy for Children (MBCT-C). Adapted from and building upon MBSR and MBCT, MBCT-C teaches mindfulness skills over a 12-week period. The sessions tend to be shorter than in the adult version since kids usually have shorter attention spans. The mindfulness exercises also tend to be shorter, and tend to be more active.

In one of the early sessions of one of our MBCT-C groups, a nine-year-old boy once said, "Today at school, the teacher made me mad, so I threw an eraser. Then she yelled at me and sent me to the principal's office. Then the principle yelled at me and sent me home. Then my parents yelled at me and sent me to my room." In other words, the young man externalized a lot of the blame for the situation.

Toward the end of the 12-week program, this same boy came into the session and said, "The other day, the teacher was talking about something I didn't like, and it made me mad. And I noticed I was getting mad. I felt my jaw get tight, and I felt my heart pounding, and I said to myself, 'I'm mad right now, so I better not say anything to the teacher. I'm gonna tell my mom when I get home.'" In my mind, it did not matter whether or not this young man had any idea what the word mindfulness meant. I considered him a success for attending this group, because in that moment, he noticed what was happening and made a conscious choice rather than an unconscious reaction (Sears, Luberto, & Sell-Smith, 2016).

The MBCT-C curriculum also teaches children how to get better at recognizing "choice points". One of the worksheets in this section explores the idea that there are many points throughout the day in which a conscious choice can be made, instead of falling back into automatic patterns of thinking, reacting, and behaving.

Tips for Working with the Practice of Noticing

When working with children with anxiety, it can be helpful for them *to practice noticing* what is happening in the moment with their five senses. As discussed earlier, this has the effect of filling their attention channels, making it more difficult for their attention to spiral off with worries and ruminations of other times and places.

There are many practices for noticing with children. They can practice mindfully peeling and eating an orange, which engages all five senses. You can ask them to bring in and play their favorite music, and ask them to pay attention to the thoughts, feelings, and sensations it brings up for them. Kids may be asked to close their eyes and identify objects by touch or by smell as a way of practicing paying attention in the moment. Children can also mindfully draw or doodle.

Since understanding judgments can be challenging for children, this too can be presented as an exercise for practicing noticing (Semple & Lee, 2011). Kids can be shown an object or a picture, and then be asked to talk about it. When a word or phrase is given, the facilitator simply asks the children to notice what they did. For example, if a child says, "It's gross!", the facilitator asks, "Okay, is 'gross' a description or a judgment?", and the child recognizes it is a judgment. If someone says, "It's sticky," they understand that they are giving a description. This can spark a discussion about the difference between descriptions and judgments. Children are taught that judgments are not necessarily bad, but if we don't know we're making them all the time, they can create problems for us.

Of course, in addition to being able to model mindfulness themselves, therapists must have good foundational training in working with children, with the skill and understanding to meet each child at the appropriate cognitive and emotional developmental level. When teaching mindfulness in a group format such as MBCT-C, it is important to make sure the participants are at a similar developmental level. Therapists must also have a good understanding of child psychopathology, in order to distinguish anxiety from other root issues like trauma or bipolar disorder.

The two worksheets that follow can help children better understand anxiety, and can help them understand and notice choice points.

When Anxiety Sneaks up on You

Anxiety is something everybody feels sometimes. Your brain is trying to send you a message to pay attention, and it makes your heart beat faster, tells your stomach to stop eating, and gives energy to your muscles. We usually only want that when we need to run away from danger, but if you worry about stuff a lot inside your head, your brain might think you still need more energy.

Anxiety can feel uncomfortable, but it won't really hurt you. It's your own brain trying to help. You can tell yourself, "Thank you for trying to help me brain, but right now I'm just _____ (sitting in class, walking down the street, or whatever you are doing). Sometimes your brain will listen, and sometimes it won't, but fighting with the anxiety only makes it worse.

Fighting with your own thoughts also can make them worse. Have you ever seen a snow globe? It is a water-filled glass container with little white flecks inside, and when you shake it up, it looks like it is snowing. Your mind is a lot like a snow globe. The more you fight with it, the more you shake it up, the worse it gets. Just practice letting it be still, and the thoughts will settle down, just like the snow settles down on the ground if you leave it alone.

Anxiety can be sneaky, like a cat creeping up slowly when it tries to catch a mouse. Even though anxiety can feel like it pounces on you, you probably did not notice it when it was sneaking. You can learn to watch the anxiety rising, like water filling you up. When you notice it sooner, you might be able to keep it from getting worse. First, let's be scientists and try to investigate the anxiety. Write down your answers to the questions below. Ask an adult if you need help.

What clues tell you that anxiety is sneaking up on you?

_____
_____
_____
_____

When you are anxious, what thoughts pop into your head?

_____
_____
_____
_____

When you are anxious, what do you feel in your body?

_____
_____
_____
_____

When anxiety comes, instead of fighting with it, you can practice making friends with it. Just feel it in your body, and thank your body and brain for trying to help. You can also pay more attention to what is around you. What do you see? What do you hear? What do you feel? What do you smell? What do you taste? Look at a beautiful tree, or pet an animal, or take a walk so your brain knows that everything is really okay.

What helps you when you start to feel anxious?

_____
_____
_____
_____

Talking to people can also help the anxiety calm down. Who can you talk to when you start getting upset?

_____

_____

_____

_____

☙❦

Remember that it is okay to have whatever thoughts or feelings you are having. Sometimes you might need to hold them in for a little while, like when you are sitting in class, but you really can't control them. You can only control what you do. You don't have to fight with your thoughts and feelings, because they belong to you! Just like the sky is sometimes sunny and sometimes stormy, you are sometimes happy and sometimes anxious. Fighting the weather won't change it. Just take care of yourself when the storm comes – it won't last forever.

Noticing Choice Points

Sometimes it's hard being a kid. There are lots of rules, and you don't always know what they are. Lots of adults tell you what to do. Sometimes we get really mad and do things that are not so good, and sometimes we get in trouble when we don't think it's really our fault.

Some people go their whole lives blaming everybody else for what happens to them. They say all their problems are their parents' fault, or their teachers' fault, or their friends' fault. That may actually be true. But you know what? **YOU are the one most in charge of your own life. You cannot control other people. You can only control yourself.** At any point, you can make a choice about what you want to do, no matter what other people are doing or saying.

You also can't control what you think and how you feel, but you can control what you do. You can control the choices you make. Thoughts and feelings can give you information, but they are not the boss of you. At any point, you can make a choice, no matter what your thoughts or feelings are telling you.

It takes practice to notice these "choice points." Use the worksheet below to help you find them more often. Ask an adult if you need help.

Think back to the last time you got in trouble for something. What happened? Who was there?

_____

_____

_____

_____

_____

What were you thinking at the time? Before the event? After the event?

_____

_____

_____

_____

_____

What were you feeling at the time? Before the event? After the event?

_____

_____

_____

_____

_____

What did you do before, during, and after the event? What helped, and what made things worse?

_____

_____

_____

_____

_____

If you could go back in time, what would you do differently? What different choices would you have made?

_____

_____

_____

_____

_____

_____

❧

Practice paying attention more to the choice points in your day. When you make a good choice, you can make things better instead of worse.

Of course, when bad things happen, it is not always your fault. It is never okay for somebody to hit you, or hurt you, or yell at you, or be mean to you. It is good to figure out the people in your life you can trust, and tell them right away if someone is being mean to you. Below, write down a list of people you can trust, like parents, grandparents, relatives, teachers, counselors, or friends.

_____

_____

_____

_____

_____

Part 5

Tools for
Mood Disorders and Depression

Mood disorders affect almost all human beings on the planet, either directly by suffering from it themselves, or indirectly by witnessing a friend or family member go through it. As pervasive as mood disorders are, assessing a client's medical and substance use history is particularly crucial. For example, I once had a client who was doing all the right things in therapy, but not getting better. As a nurse, she began doing her own research on the medications she was taking, and discovered that depression was a potential side effect of the beta-blocker she was on. She had a very difficult time withdrawing from the medication, but when she did, her depressive symptoms began to lift almost immediately.

Depression has been called the "common cold" of mental health. Far beyond the normal experience of feeling sad, major depressive disorder significantly impact's an individual's daily functioning. Even though depression is very common, it can be challenging for many professionals to treat. These disorders hijack clients' thinking patterns, and their ongoing negativity and pessimism can make them difficult to be around. Progress can also be very slow for someone with depression, and it may take weeks or months to show improvement.

Severe episodes of depression can even create psychotic symptoms. Mood congruent hallucinations are related to depressive themes like death. When I worked on acute psychiatric inpatient units, one woman told me she could see skeletons around her. Another patient told me he could see blood dripping from the walls.

Decades ago, Aaron Beck identified three negative thinking patterns that always accompany a person with clinical depression. You will never meet someone suffering from depression who has high self-esteem, a positive outlook on the world, or hope for the future. If you do, they are not likely in the throes of a major depressive episode.

These thinking styles matter. That's because individuals with a negative view of self believe they are terrible people, they cannot do anything right, and that they are inherently flawed. They often also feel strong guilt for their faults, real or perceived. Those with a negative view of the world feel they cannot trust anyone, and that no one will ever help them. They may believe that the whole world is "going to hell in a hand basket," and that it is not a safe place. Finally, individuals with a negative view of the future think that things will never get better, and that things will keep getting worse. In severe depression, there is often a foreshortening of a sense of the future. The client may have difficulty even imagining the next five minutes, much less five years into the future.

These three ways of thinking obviously lead clients to feel a sense of hopelessness, and this often triggers suicidal ideation.

TIPS FOR WORKING WITH SUICIDAL IDEATION

For many therapists, their biggest fear is of a client committing suicide. Approximately 25% of therapists will have a client who suicides over the course of their careers (McAdams & Foster, 2000). While it can be very stressful if it does happen to you, considering how many clients we see over the years, the odds of it happening with any given client are fairly low. Clients who really want to commit suicide will probably not seek professional help. Those who seek out therapists are typically trying to find a way to keep living.

I'm certainly not saying that you shouldn't take suicidal ideation seriously, but that you have to work through your own discomfort and do what is best for the client. Many therapists work on a CYA (cover your @$$) basis, and react based on fear. For example, many agencies require clients to sign a safety plan, despite the fact that the research shows that they do not make any difference (McMyler, & Pryjmachuk, 2008; Rudd, Mandrusiak, & Joiner, 2006).

In her review of the literature, Marsha Linehan found no evidence that inpatient hospitalization is more therapeutic or keeps people alive longer than a good outpatient program (Hewer & Linehan, 2015). While I would certainly not tell therapists never to send clients to the hospital, it takes training and experience to tease out our own fears from what is best for the client. Marsha Linehan has also expressed the urgent need for more training for our graduate students. I was fortunate enough to receive a great deal of supervised experience working with individuals who were suicidal. One of the rotations on my internship was in a rural setting, where I was one of the few providers available, and I was often called for mental health crises. I clearly remember receiving phone calls from physicians along the lines of, "Hello. I have a patient here in my office who says he is going to go to Wal-Mart, buy a shotgun, kill his family, and then kill himself. The Sheriff is going to drive him over to your office." While you never get completely comfortable with such serious situations, over time, you learn to get past your own fears and do what is in the best interests of the client.

When assessing suicidality, a commonly used acronym is "SLAP," which stands for **S**pecificity of the plan, **L**ethality of the method, **A**vailability of the method, and **P**roximity of helping resources (Miller, 1985; Sommers-Flanagan & Sommers-Flanagan, 1995). If you are unfamiliar with "SLAP," I recommend you learn more about it, as well as other methods for working with suicidality.

Though the subject can make therapists uncomfortable, clients seem to appreciate it when we can express our empathy and understanding of why the client is considering suicide. Here is an example of how to address this with clients:

> *"You just told me that you feel terrible about yourself, you think the world is an awful place, and that it feels like it will never get better. To your mind, things probably seem pretty hopeless. I'll bet the thought of not feeling anything probably feels pretty attractive to you right now. Maybe that thought surprised you or scared you. Maybe the thoughts have been around so long they seem like old friends.*
>
> > *However, the real problem is that you are depressed. Depression hijacks your thinking. People who are depressed tell themselves they are no good, and they feel like things will never get better. You might even think to yourself, 'I thought it was just me who thought I was a terrible person.' Well, guess what, you thinking it is just you is a symptom of depression. The real problem is the depression, which we can definitely treat. If you can hang in there a little while, and postpone the permanent solution of escape through suicide, there are proven treatments for depression."*

In general, it is important to develop a safety plan with the client. Can they stay, or at least regularly check in, with a close friend or family member? Would they be willing to call you or a crisis intervention line if the thoughts get more intense? Given that the real problem is the depression, help them develop a plan to take care of themselves for the times they are feeling more depressed.

The following handout may be helpful for clients to better understand depression.

Understanding Depression

All of us experience times in our lives when we are "down," "blue," or "in a funk." For many people, this does not last long, and goes away after a few days, or after taking a break, or after doing something they enjoy doing.

However, in major depressive disorder, these feelings are much more intense, and last for at least two weeks. People with clinical depression are likely to experience most of the following symptoms nearly every day:

- Feeling sad, empty, hopeless, or irritable most of the day.
- Things that used to be fun no longer bring pleasure.
- Significant changes in appetite or weight.
- Sleeping too much or too little.
- Feeling agitated, or moving slowly.

- A significant loss of energy.
- Strong feelings of worthlessness or guilt.
- Difficulty thinking and making decisions.
- Thoughts of death or suicide.

It is common for people to experience these symptoms from time to time, especially when experiencing significant loss or crises. However, in major depressive disorder, these symptoms take on a life of their own, and seriously interfere with your ability to function in your life, work, and relationships.

Unless they've been clinically depressed themselves, your friends and family will probably not understand. They will tell you to "just get over it," or "work harder," or "pull yourself up by your own bootstraps." This contributes to the sense that there is something wrong with you, or that it is somehow your fault.

People with depression tend to experience a constant stream of negative thoughts. Depression hijacks your thinking in three ways:

1) First of all, it sparks negative thoughts about yourself, such as, "There is something wrong with me," or "I'm a terrible person," or "I'm unlovable."

2) Depression also creates thoughts that the world is an unsafe place, that people are uncaring, and that nobody will ever help you.

3) The third way depression alters your thinking is that it robs you of a sense of the future. When you are deeply depressed, you cannot even imagine five minutes from now, much less five years from now. If you do think about the future, it will seem like things will only get worse, and that there is no hope that things will ever get better. Because of these worries, it is also common to experience anxiety along with the depression.

Because your thinking itself becomes hijacked, it is very important to get the outside perspective and help of a therapist or counselor. Only an experienced mental health professional can determine if you have clinical depression.

BEHAVIORAL ACTIVATION

Recent research suggests that all bona fide models of psychotherapy are equally effective in the treatment of depression (Abbass & Town, 2016). However, the key ingredient is behavioral activation. This is important, because although depression will often pass by itself after a few months, clients can inadvertently do things to perpetuate it, such as withdrawing from meaningful activities and isolating themselves. For that reason, the crucial component in recovery from depression is that the client needs to get moving.

You may have brilliant insights into how the depression got started, or why it is continuing, or even the family dynamics that took place during childhood that contributed to it, but somehow all of that has to translate into clients becoming more active in their lives. It may be simply getting out of bed, or walking around the block, or going out to be around other people. In fact, physical exercise is now considered an evidence-based intervention for depression (Deslandes, 2015; Rosenbaum, Tiedemann, Ward, Curtis, & Sherrington, 2015).

Here's the hard sell -- a client experiencing depression will not feel like doing those activities, and they will not feel better right away. This is why it can be very helpful to get the support and encouragement of friends and family. It is also important for clients to get more in touch with their life values, so they feel some motivation to get better.

The worksheet that follows will help clients engage in activating and getting themselves moving again.

Surviving Depression

If you have been diagnosed with major depressive disorder, you are probably not very hopeful that things will get better. After all, feeling down and hopeless is a symptom of depression. Because of how strongly it affects your thinking, emotions, and your sense of self, major depressive disorder can be difficult to recover from on your own.

Remember that depression hijacks your thinking. If you have a thought, "I am a terrible person," that is the depression talking. Things may even seem so bad at times that you have thoughts that you do not want to go on living. It's normal to have that thought, because things seem so bad to your mind, but once again, that is the depression talking. If the thoughts are frequent and strong, talk to a professional right away, or go to your nearest emergency room. If you live in the United States, you can call the National Suicide Hotline at 1-800-273-TALK (8255).

The good news is that there are now a number of well-researched, effective treatments for depression. Talk to a professional about which options might work best for you.

First of all, make sure you are receiving good medical care. Symptoms of depression can be caused by, or made worse by, your body and brain chemistry, such as thyroid and vitamin D levels. Sometimes medications have side effects that mimic depression, and some medical diseases contribute to depressive symptoms.

Also, take an honest look at any substances that might contribute to your depression. Alcohol and tranquilizers can make depression worse, and caffeine or energy drinks can contribute to feelings of anxiety.

Some people find antidepressant medication helpful, and recent studies have shown that taking Omega-3 can be effective. Some people use light therapy, in which they expose themselves to bright light to stimulate the brain. In some serious cases, doctors may recommend electrical or magnetic stimulation of the brain.

Psychotherapy, or talking with a professional psychologist, counselor, or social worker, has been proven beneficial, and can also teach you skills for preventing future issues. There are different types of psychotherapy, and most of them have been shown to be equally effective, so you may be able to choose the approach that best suits you by first asking potential therapists about what they do.

The most important thing in recovering from clinical depression is called "behavioral activation." **That's just a fancy way of saying, "get moving."** It does not matter much if you intellectually understand why you are depressed, or what is keeping you depressed. Normally, we wait for our thoughts and emotions to tell us when we "feel like" doing something. With depression, we need to do the opposite. When you are depressed, you cannot trust your thoughts and feelings, so don't listen to them. You also don't need to fight with them, or argue with yourself. Just notice the thoughts and feelings, and get moving.

The scientific benefits of exercise on depression and general mental health have been known for decades, but at the very least, do the following:

- Get out of bed or off the couch
- Take a walk around the block
- Go out to the store or to a park
- Do things with friends or family members
- Engage in a hobby that you used to enjoy

Your brain will tell you that it won't make a difference. You will probably not feel like doing those things, because depression robs you of your ability to feel pleasure. You probably won't even feel better after you do the activity, but do it anyway, and the feelings will catch up later.

In the spaces below, write down a plan to help you survive this episode of depression. Answer the following questions:

What activities can you do, however small, to get yourself moving and active?

_____

_____

What hobbies can you do, even if you don't enjoy them at first?

_____

_____

What professionals, friends, and family members can support you through this?

_____

_____

How can you take care of yourself during this difficult period?

_____

_____

❧

Because your mind is not in a good place right now, make sure you seek help in creating and enacting your plan.

PREVENTING DEPRESSIVE RELAPSE

Getting stuck in "brain grooves," relapse is a serious problem for those suffering from major depressive disorder. The more often a person gets depressed, the more likely they are to get depressed again. After suffering two episodes of Major Depressive Disorder, clients have a 70 to 80 percent chance of relapsing into depression yet again (Keller, Lavori, Lewis, & Klerman, 1983; Kupfer, 1991).

Mindfulness-Based Cognitive Therapy (MBCT) was originally designed to specifically deal with this issue. The developers of MBCT began as depression researchers. Their very important research question was, "How do we prevent depression from coming back?" The interventions that were already being done, including pharmacotherapy, were not doing a very good job of preventing future episodes. The researchers were keen to find an effective prophylactic treatment, ideally one that was time-limited and could be delivered in a group format.

Of course, as good researchers, they had to first determine what causes people to relapse into depression, then design an intervention to interrupt those causes. What they found was that clients who had previously experienced depression took significantly longer to recover from a even a small dip in mood as compared to someone who had never been depressed. While it is normal to have ups and downs in mood, if someone has been depressed before, it will take longer to recover from that dip, and that is when the client is at risk.

When the mood dips, a depressive cycle begins. Clients tend to withdraw from activities, which tends to increase their sadness. The more the mood lowers, the more negative thoughts are activated again, and the more the mood dips. Clients do not usually go quickly from being perfectly fine to being clinically depressed. It tends to come on gradually as their mood slowly declines.

Since mindfulness is about paying attention, the developers of MBCT found it to be a very useful tool in the prevention of depression. Clients are taught to notice and accept the reality of the earliest signs, and to take preventive action, even though they may not feel like it. Rather than getting caught up in depressing thoughts, they decenter from them, and see them as a sign that the depression is returning. It is much easier to take action in the early stages to prevent the depression from worsening than it is to pull oneself out of the pit of a major depressive episode.

MBCT has been studied with well-controlled clinical research, demonstrating significant reductions in depressive relapse rates, especially for those who have suffered three or more previous major depressive episodes (Hofmann, Sawyer, Witt, & Oh, 2010; Kuyken, Crane, & Dalgleish, 2012; Ma & Teasdale, 2004; Piet & Hougaard, 2011; Segal, Teasdale, & Williams, 2004; Teasdale, Segal, & Williams, 1995; Teasdale, Segal, Williams, Ridgeway, Soulsby, & Lau, 2000; Williams & Kuyken, 2012). MBCT has also been shown to be as effective as maintenance antidepressant pharmacotherapy (Kuyken, Byford, Byng, Dalgleish, Lewis, et al, 2010; Segal, Bieling, Young, McQueen, Cooke, et. al., 2010).

A mindfulness approach helps clients explore how their daily activities impact the likelihood of their depression returning. Clients are often surprised when they fully recognize that they are engaged in draining activities all day long, and seldom engage in self-care, which puts them at risk. Developing a personalized relapse prevention plan helps clients take proactive steps before they become overwhelmed by the oncoming depression.

In the following worksheet, clients can begin the process of learning how to be proactive at preventing depressive relapse.

Why Depression Keeps Coming Back, and How to Prevent It

If you've had depression before, you know what a horrible experience it is. How it robs you of your thinking, your emotions, and your sense of the future. How it affects everything in your life, like your work and your relationships.

Sadly, clinical research has found that every time you have an episode of major depressive disorder, your chances of getting it again goes up. If you have suffered two previous episodes of clinical depression, your chances of getting depressed again jumps up to almost 80 percent. Some people struggle with depression their whole lives, seemingly caught in a vicious cycle.

The good news is that research has discovered why depression keeps coming back, and how to prevent future episodes. Basically, your brain creates certain patterns based on your experiences. If you've been depressed in the past, your brain has sort of a "depression groove" that you can keep falling back into.

All of us have ups and downs in mood on a daily basis. However, if you've been depressed before, and you have even a small dip in mood, it will take you longer to pull out of that dip compared to people who have never been depressed. When your mood is down, you are at risk for gradually spiraling down even further.

For example, let's say you had dinner plans with a friend tonight, but right now, you are feeling a little down, so you decide to cancel and stay home. Sometimes we all need to take a break and stay home, but watch out for this becoming a pattern. When you stay home, you feel a little more lonely, which makes you a little more sad. Because you feel more sad, you definitely don't want to go out tomorrow night. After staying home two nights in a row, you feel even more sad, which starts to activate some negative thoughts, like, "I'm such a loser for just staying home alone," which makes your mood drop even more.

Depression tends to come on gradually like this, rather than all at once, if you pay attention. People usually don't want to acknowledge the reality that depression is coming back, since it is such a horrible thing to go through. So, they tend to ignore it, or push themselves harder, which only makes them feel more tired and more depressed.

If you can pay attention to the oncoming warning signs, you can take action to prevent a full episode of depression from coming back. Even though you will not like realizing it might be coming back, it is much easier and much more effective to take action early, before you slide all the way down into the deep pit of depression.

Use the space below to write down your own warning signs that the depression is returning. What kinds of thoughts start popping up in your mind? What emotions start coming up? What do you feel in your body? What do you tend to do (for example, sleep too much, watch a lot of TV, stay home more, worry about problems constantly, etc.)?

_____

_____

Once you notice the warning signs, it is important to take action. Some people withdraw and give up on doing things altogether, in the hope that their unpleasant thoughts and emotions, or the things they need to deal with, will be "out of sight, out of mind." Unfortunately, this strategy works only temporarily at best.

It's good to have a plan when the depression starts coming back, because when the depression grows stronger, you may not feel like doing anything. Make a promise to yourself to create a list below, and to do something on that list whether you feel like it or not when the symptoms start to show up again.

What specific things can you do to take care of yourself when you see the signs of depression coming on? For example, call your therapist (if you don't have one, get one!), talk to a friend or family member, write your feelings down on paper to get some perspective on them, take a relaxing bath, do a hobby, take a walk, exercise, etc.

_____

_____

Since depression robs you of motivation, it may be hard to do the above things, even when you know it will help. In the space below, write down your reasons for wanting to stay mentally healthy. What is important to you? What makes your life more fulfilling? You may wish to start with broad categories, like family, relationships, spirituality, learning, career, etc. Take some time to ponder these questions since things often don't seem that important once the depression takes hold of you.

_____

_____

※

When depression creeps in, your automatic impulse may be to get lost in your head, and worry about all of your problems, or about other people, or about the future. Sometimes that can be helpful, but when you notice that you are not really fixing anything by worrying, don't forget to keep asking yourself, "What do I need to do right now to take care of *myself*?" Bring your attention back to the present, and just take things one moment at a time.

Ideally, make some time every day to take care of yourself, and remind yourself of what really matters to you. If you can add more self-care on a regular basis, and stay focused on what you value most in life, you may be able to prevent depression from even starting to come back.

BIPOLAR DISORDER

Bipolar disorder, formerly known as manic-depression, is characterized by periods of depression and periods of mania or hypomania. Individuals with bipolar I disorder experience both manic episodes and major depressive episodes. Those with bipolar II disorder experience major depressive episodes and hypomanic episodes. Cyclothymic disorder involves alternating periods of depressive and hypomanic symptoms, which last at least two years in adults or one year for children, and do not meet the full criteria for hypomanic or major depressive episodes (American Psychiatric Association, 2012).

Modern society tends to reward hypomanic behavior, since the energy allows people to sleep less and get more work done. Many clients feel good when experiencing hypomania, so may have little motivation to change or prevent it. Some clients claim that mood stabilizers leave them feeling flat, and they would rather have the excitement of the ups and downs of mood. The important question for clients is how they do when they are not on medication. If they end up damaging important relationships for example, perhaps they would be willing to feel a little flatter in order to live a more fulfilling life.

There are a number of other common comorbid conditions that occur with bipolar I disorder. Anxiety disorders occur in three-fourths of these individuals. ADHD, impulse-control, and conduct disorders occur in over half of these clients. They also have higher rates of co-occurring medical conditions, such as metabolic syndrome and migraines (American Psychiatric Association, 2012).

As with all disorders, make sure the client is receiving appropriate medical care, with checks on such systems as hormone and endocrine functioning. It is especially important to assess for substance use and abuse, a comorbid condition in over half of individuals with bipolar I disorder (American Psychiatric Association, 2012). Clients may self-medicate with uppers like methamphetamines or high doses of caffeine and/or downers like benzodiazepines or alcohol.

In assessing for bipolar disorder, be sure to rule out mood swings based on other factors, like personality disorders, PTSD, medical issues, the effects of substances, or normal reactions to abnormal life circumstances. When I worked on an inpatient unit, I encountered a patient who was misdiagnosed as bipolar when actually he had experienced a brief period of excitement after winning the lottery, followed by a gambling trip to Vegas and staying up late with friends. All of this left him exhausted and sleeping for days after his return home!

Mindfulness-based cognitive therapy has been successfully adapted for working with individuals with bipolar disorder. Reminiscent of the Dialectical Behavior Therapy approach, MBCT for Bipolar Disorder suggests having both didactic skill-building groups as well as individual psychotherapy sessions.

MBCT-C has also been used with children and adolescents at risk for developing bipolar disorder, who had mood dysregulation and anxiety disorders, and initial results look quite promising (Cotton, Luberto, Sears, Strawn, Wasson, & DelBello, 2015; Sears, Bruns, Cotton, DelBello, Strawn, et al., 2017; Semple & Lee, 2011; Strawn, Cotton, Luberto, Patino, Stahl, et al., 2016).

The following worksheet may be helpful for clients who have been diagnosed with bipolar disorder, especially for understanding manic episodes. It may also be helpful to give clients handouts on depression, anxiety, or addiction, as needed.

Living with
Bipolar Disorder

If you've been diagnosed with bipolar disorder, you've experienced significant mood swings that have significantly interfered with your life and relationships.

Sometimes, people feel like they don't need medication when they start to feel better, or they just stop taking it because they think they don't really have bipolar disorder. However, stopping medication has the potential of causing serious problems. Always talk to your doctor before changing your medication levels or stopping it. If you don't agree with your doctor about your diagnosis, talk about the reasons you disagree. If you really feel like you need to, it might be useful to go see another doctor for a second opinion, but frequent doctor jumping is usually not helpful.

Since bipolar disorder can disrupt your mood and your thinking, it can be useful to get outside help. Mental health professionals can provide a safe place to get perspective on and work wisely with distressing thoughts and feelings. Medical providers can prescribe stabilizing medication, and can make sure that there aren't any underlying medical issues contributing to your mood changes.

It is also important to pay attention to the substances you use, since they can have a big impact on mood. If you feel that you must drink alcohol, caffeine, or energy drinks, check with your provider about how much is okay to partake of each day.

No one likes to feel depression, so it will be obvious to you when it comes back, and you will definitely want to feel better when it creeps in. But what about mania? Where is the line between feeling good and feeling *too* good?

It's okay to feel happy, and you should give yourself permission to enjoy feeling happy. However, as you have experienced, during a manic episode your mood goes abnormally high, or you feel extremely anxious or irritable, creating problems in your life, work, and relationships. Sometimes it's hard to be aware of how bad things are getting when you're in the middle of the episode, so it can be useful to reflect back on previous episodes to be better prepared in case the symptoms start to return.

NOTICING THE WARNING SIGNS

Below is a list of common signs and symptoms of a manic or hypomanic episode:

- Super high self-esteem
- Can't seem to stop moving
- Can't sleep, or don't need to sleep more than a few hours a night
- Easily distracted
- Talking fast
- Endless flurry of thoughts and ideas

- Making bad decisions
- Feeling invincible when doing dangerous things
- Risky sexual behavior
- Excessive shopping sprees

Think back to any previous manic episodes that you can remember. What were the initial signs that things were going from just feeling good to mania?

_____

_____

_____

Were there any environmental triggers or stressors at the time? Were there specific events, situations, or people associated with the oncoming symptoms?

_____

_____

_____

What thoughts or thinking patterns begin to creep up when the mania is coming back, and how do they change as things get worse?

_____

_____

_____

What feelings or emotions are associated with oncoming mania, and how do they change as the episode progresses?

_____

_____

_____

Are there any signs in your physical body? Do you notice any patterns of sensations in your body when mania creeps in? If so, in what specific places do you notice them? Do they change with time?

_____

_____

_____

_____

What were some of the early behavioral signs? What things did you start to do (or not do) that were not normal for you? How did those behaviors change as the mania got worse?

_____

_____

_____

COSTS

I don't have to tell you that the symptoms of bipolar disorder can wreak havoc on your life. What problems have you dealt with, and continue to deal with? What has been the cost of struggling with your illness? What important things have you been doing less of in your life, or even given up completely?

_____

_____

_____

VALUES

What reasons do you have to stay healthy? What do you value in life? What is important enough to you that you would be willing to go through the discomfort of getting help or doing the work of staying healthy, or even the discomfort of making room in your life for your symptoms when they aren't going away?

_____

_____

_____

WHEN THE SIGNS ARE THERE

Now that you have clear reasons for wanting to be healthy, when the warning signs you have identified above begin to creep up, what concrete, practical things can you do to prevent your mood from getting worse? What has helped and not helped in the past? It may be difficult to think of these things when you are not feeling well, so keep this list handy. Examples of action steps could include calling your doctor, talking to a friend, journaling, taking a walk, exercising, listening to music, or doing a hobby.

_____

_____

_____

_____

TAKING CARE OF YOURSELF LONG TERM

Perhaps the most important thing you can do to stay healthy is to proactively take care of yourself to prevent future problems. What do you do now to take care of yourself? What would you like to do more of? Are there things you can change, even if only gradually, to reduce some of the stress in your life? What do you do, or would like to do more, just for fun? What hobbies do you enjoy?

_____

_____

_____

_____

_____

_____

_____

_____

GETTING SOCIAL SUPPORT

Having the right support can be very helpful in living with bipolar disorder. For one thing, it can be useful to get an outside perspective on how you seem to be doing from an objective observer who knows what is "normal" for you. Friends, family, counselors, and spiritual advisors can also be there for you when you need help, and can provide that sense of connection and belonging that keeps stress down. Who can you count on for help when you need it?

_____

_____

_____

_____

_____

_____

_____

_____

Part 6

Tools for Challenging Issues

When working with "challenging" clients, always remember that even the most difficult clients are just human beings going through very significant issues. As the saying goes, but for grace and circumstances, there go I. It is important to remind ourselves that all human experiences and disorders lie on a continuum. I find it helpful to remind myself that if my genetics, life experiences, or brain chemistry had been different, I might be in exactly the place my client is now.

Our own personal mindfulness practices as clinicians may well be the most important factor, so that we can stay present with the most challenging clients, and meet them where they are.

TIPS FOR WORKING WITH THE STAGES OF CHANGE

When we are working with clients who do not seem to be getting better, it may well be because we are not assessing their stage of readiness for change, and are not meeting them where they are. Research has shown that there are stages of change clients go through, and action is considered the fourth stage (Prochaska, 1999; Prochaska & DiClemente, 1992; Prochaska, DiClemente, & Norcross, 1992). It is important to assess which stage of change the client is in, and to start from there. Clients can of course be in multiple stages at once sometimes, or can be in different stages for different issues, but understanding the stages of change can be very useful clinically (Prochaska & Norcross, 2010).

For example, pushing clients to take action before they are ready can be counterproductive. Over time, this can lead to therapists becoming burned out and even cynical about their clients' lack of progress. Recognizing where a client is at in the process of change and helping them understand that is an important first step. Let's look briefly at the Stages of Change.

Pre-contemplation

In this stage, the client is not even aware of the areas that need changing. They may be caught up in old, automatic patterns of reacting to everyone around them and are likely to blame everyone else for their problems. The most important thing to do at this point is to help them become more aware of what is actually going on, and help raise awareness.

Contemplation

In the contemplation stage, clients are "thinking about it." They are somewhat aware of the impact of their own choices and behaviors, but are still getting some kind of benefit from the way they are now. At this point, the therapist can help the client weigh the pros and cons of changing or staying the same.

Preparation

At this point, clients intellectually know they need to change, but are not quite ready to take action. Many clients feel like they need to "get ready" for change. This may be a psychological readiness, like writing out actual plans, mentally getting up the energy, or grieving the loss of old habits. It may also be a physical preparation, like putting into place a modified environment to make it easier to make the change happen.

Action

When they realize what they are doing is causing a problem, and they see more benefit in changing over staying the same, and they have prepared themselves, now clients are finally ready to actually take action and make the changes they desire to make. They can put the plan into effect.

Maintenance

The maintenance stage is crucial because it is very easy for people to slip back into older patterns that they may have been doing for a lifetime, especially during times of stress. Changes are very rarely done once and for always. It can be important to pay attention and watch for the signs of relapse and falling back into old habits. It may even be necessary to go back through and revisit some of the other stages in order to revise one's plan and take different actions to maintain the change.

ADDICTIONS

Addiction is a serious problem in modern society, and it can take many forms. Substance use disorders occur with both prescription drugs and illicit substances. Cigarettes, alcohol, and in many states now, marijuana, are legal and even socially acceptable. People can also become trapped in addictive behaviors, like gambling, eating, and sex. Technological advances have increased computer gaming and Internet pornography addictions. Prescription drugs like Adderall and Oxycodone are prone to abuse. In addition, dangerous drugs like crystal meth and heroin are becoming increasingly available and deadly.

As with all mental health disorders, it is important to remember that addictive behaviors lie on a continuum. We all have addictions to various degrees, whether to a morning cup of coffee, a work routine, or a comfortable bed. Individuals with addictions can sometimes be very manipulative and selfish in their behaviors, but at the root of this, they are human beings who want to be happy and escape from their suffering. They have simply become trapped in a vicious circle. Our challenge is to accept the human being even if we do not condone the behaviors.

The view of addiction has changed a lot over the years. When I first received training in addictions, I had a few supervisors who still believed that the therapist needed to metaphorically beat people over the head to make them feel bad, so they would quit using. The therapist might even berate them for all the terrible things they had been doing to themselves and their families. However, this tended to backfire. What do people with an addiction do when they feel bad? They want to go back to their addictive behaviors to feel better. Given that average relapse rates are between 40-60% (McLellan, Lewis, O'Brien, & Kleber, 2000), it is almost inevitable that clients are going to slip sometimes, and if they are made to feel bad for it, they will not come back to therapy. This is known as the "abstinence violation effect," which I call the "f@#k-it" effect, in which the person just decides to go back to using after they slip.

Newer approaches to working with addictions incorporate the stages of change model discussed above (Prochaska, DiClemente, & Norcross, 1992) and the principles of motivational interviewing (Miller & Rollnick, 2013). Therapists who use motivational interviewing (1) express empathy through reflective listening, (2) develop discrepancy between clients' goals or values and their current behavior, (3) avoid argument and direct confrontation, (4) adjust to client resistance rather than opposing it directly, and (5) support self-efficacy and optimism. In short, motivational interviewing addresses clients' ambivalence about change.

The truth is, everyone already knows how to quit. If you want to quit smoking, all you have to do is not touch any cigarettes to your lips. What's the real question? The real question is, "How do I tolerate these urges, these cravings, these uncomfortable emotions?" Since the substance or addictive behavior lowers craving or anxiety almost immediately, the behavior is negatively reinforced. Clients want desperately to avoid these uncomfortable feelings, so it can be very challenging to break out of this cycle of negative reinforcement.

An eight-week group intervention, based upon MBSR and MBCT, is showing great promise in clinical research. Known as Mindfulness-Based Relapse Prevention (MBRP: Bowen, Chawla, & Marlatt, 2011), it makes use of motivational interviewing, CBT, and mindfulness principles. An important component of MBRP is known as "urge surfing," which teaches clients to ride out the sensations they are experiencing.

Tips for Working with Urge Surfing

The urge surfing principle used in MBRP is similar to the concept of riding out the sensations of anxiety, as described in the Moving into the Swimming Pool handout in Part 3. Normally when cravings arise, clients try to get rid of them through engaging in the addiction or by doing something to distract themselves. Remember that distraction is a useful tool at times, but if it is the only tool, it can set up a cycle of avoidance and struggle.

While it can be challenging and uncomfortable, clients can learn to more directly experience the physical sensations of craving, and learn to "surf" the waves of the urges, noticing how they come and go on their own, in a type of exposure therapy. Of course, urge surfing is best taught as a relapse prevention strategy after clients have been through detoxification from the substance. If a client needs an "eye opener" each morning, it is a sign of physiological dependence on alcohol, and withdrawing too quickly from it can lead to delirium tremens and even death.

In addition to learning how to manage urges and emotions, it is important not to put oneself in places or situations in which relapse is more likely to occur. Finding a new social circle can be especially challenging, as it is hard to change when your friends keep engaging in the behavior.

Since slips are inevitable on the journey to recovery, they can become learning experiences. Performing a chain analysis can help clients become more aware of what led to the slip, and help them develop new strategies to prevent future slips.

The worksheets that follow can be useful for clients to develop a relapse prevention plan and to help them perform a chain analysis if they slip.

Relapse Prevention

If you are free right now from your addiction, you have reason to celebrate. As you well know, staying free of your addiction is not easy. Though it gets easier with time, it takes proactive effort to maintain your progress. Use this worksheet to get better at noticing the triggers and warning signs of relapse, and to develop your own personalized relapse prevention plan.

First of all, describe the addiction you have struggled with. What is it? When and how did it start? What did you get from it? How bad did it get? What were the costs of the addiction? What people or things did you lose?

_____

_____

What are your personal triggers? Take some time to think of all the things that can spark your desire to go back to your addiction, such as specific situations, places, people, thoughts, emotions, and memories.

_____

_____

When craving starts to rear its ugly head, what are the first signs you notice?

_____

_____

What do you notice in your physical body when you have cravings? (For example, fast heartbeat, nausea, stomach churning, headaches, etc.)

_____

_____

How do those body sensations change with time? Do they start in one place and spread? Do they build up rapidly or slowly? What are the first signs that they are starting to level off and then fade away?

_____

_____

What emotions arise when you are craving? Try to discern if there are a lot of different emotions underneath the first or strongest ones that come up. How do they tend to change with time?

_____

_____

What thoughts or images pop into your mind when you are craving? Do they change with time?

_____

_____

_____

Your addiction probably made you feel better right away, but staying clean is a long-term process. Why do you want to be free of your addiction? What people, things, or activities are meaningful to you? What are your life values? What is important enough to you that you would be willing to feel some discomfort in order to have more of it in your life?

_____

_____

On a separate piece of paper, develop your own relapse prevention plan. Write out concrete actions steps that you can take when the signs and urges related to your addiction begin getting strong. It is important to note that when you are starting to get overwhelmed, you probably won't feel like doing these things, but just do them anyway. It might also be helpful to share your plan with a friend or sponsor.

Here are a few suggestions to consider:

- Call a friend, sponsor, or therapist.
- Attend a support group (Alcoholics Anonymous, Smart Recovery, Sex and Love Addicts Anonymous, etc.)
- Write down what you are thinking and feeling to get it out of your head and get perspective on it.
- Just sit and watch the urges rise and fall rather than battling with them.
- Exercise, or take a walk out in nature.
- Do a hobby, or start a new one that you used to do or that you always wanted to try.
- Do something that takes you one step closer to the people or things that are valuable in your life.

Sometimes the road to recovery seems long and challenging, but as an old Chinese proverb says, "The journey of a 1,000 miles begins with a single step." Don't get overly caught up in worrying about the future. Start with today, just this moment right now, and remember to be kind to yourself. This may well be the most challenging thing you will ever do.

Chain Analysis after a Slip

It can be really tough to break an addiction. Very few people can quit cold turkey. Almost everyone will slip on the road to recovery.

Once you have slipped, the worst thing you can do is continue to beat yourself up about it. That will only make you feel bad, and when you feel bad, it will make you want to fall back into the addiction again to try to escape the bad feelings.

All you can do is start again right now, today, in this moment. Rather than feeling helpless in the grip of your addiction, you can learn from your experiences. You can analyze the chain of events that led to the slip. You can figure out the causes, so that you can be more pro-active to prevent slips from happening again.

I once worked with a man recovering from crack cocaine addiction. He told me he did some work for a friend, so the friend gave him a ten-dollar bill to thank him. The man stuck the bill in his pocket, and felt good that he helped a friend and made a little money. He decided to go for a walk since it was a beautiful day. As he was walking, he decided to pass by his old neighborhood just to see how it might have changed. He remembered there was a house down a certain street where he used to use, so he thought he would see how it looked now. He saw someone he knew on the porch, so he thought he would say hello, and share the good news that he was doing well in recovery. The friend invited him inside to have a soda, and before he knew it, my client was smoking crack again.

When did the slip happen? Was it only in the moment when the crack pipe touched his lips? When he went inside the house? When he went up to the porch? When he walked down that certain street? When he entered his old neighborhood? When he decided to take a walk? When he had ten dollars in his pocket? Or was there something else going on, like cravings or unpleasant feelings he did not notice?

Obviously, there were many points in this scenario when this man could have made a different decision. It would be extremely hard to say no when the crack pipe was right in front of him, but much easier to decide to stay away from the old neighborhood where he knew he could get the crack for only ten dollars.

Take some time to honestly explore your last slip, using the questions to guide you.

Describe the slip incident in detail. What did you do? Who was with you?

_____

_____

_____

_____

_____

What were the chain of events that happened right before the slip? What were you doing? What were you thinking? What were you feeling? What sensations were in your body? Be sure to include everything you can think of, whether or not it seems related at first. You may begin to see patterns you did not notice before.

_____

_____

_____

What thoughts and feelings were present an hour before the slip? Earlier that day? The day before? The week before? What contributions did your thoughts and feelings have to the chain of events?

_____

_____

_____

Now that you have a better understanding of the slip, what could you do differently if the situation unfolds again? Where could you make different choices? What strategies or support might help you through such a situation in the future?

_____

_____

_____

How are you feeling right now, as you are working on this handout?

_____

_____

_____

What can you do right now to take care of yourself, so that any unpleasant feelings or cravings you might be having do not continue to grow?

_____

_____

_____

CHRONIC PAIN

When working with individuals suffering from chronic pain, it is very important not to imply that the pain is "in their heads," or that if they meditate, the pain will go away. If you do that, the client's "bullcrap detector" will go off, and they will not likely want to work with you.

By definition, pain hurts. As therapists, we may not be able to do anything about the source of a client's physical pain, but we can help them let go of some of the struggle they develop with it over time, and help them with comorbid stress, anxiety, and depression.

Mindfulness can be an effective tool to help clients relate differently to their pain. Understandably, many clients get so caught up in their struggles with pain that they stop living. Therapists can help clients rediscover and move toward what is important and meaningful in their lives, even if they have to bring the pain along for the ride.

One of the consistent research findings in using mindfulness for chronic pain is that clients report needing less pain medication. For many individuals, this outcome alone makes the practice worthwhile, so they can be more alert and more present in their lives, since many pain meds make them feel foggy and groggy.

The following worksheets may be helpful for clients to better understand and live with their chronic pain.

Living with Chronic Pain

If you have been living with chronic pain, you know how devastating it can be. It's like a monster that just won't get off your back, no matter where you go and what you do. There are times when it feels overwhelming, and perhaps times when it's not so bad. When it's not so bad, you might even start to do more, only to regret it the next day.

You may have learned to distract yourself from the pain by trying to think about or pay attention to other things so you don't have to feel the pain in your body. Distraction can be an important tool, especially during flare-ups. However, distraction takes a lot of energy, and can become more difficult to maintain over time, especially as you grow older. It can be helpful to have more tools in your toolbox.

Someone once said, "pain x resistance = suffering." Because pain is so uncomfortable, we tend to fight with our own bodies, which has the long-term tendency to only increase our suffering. You likely have very real medical reasons why you are feeling so much pain. Hopefully, you will be able to continue working with your medical providers to reduce your pain as much as possible.

Unfortunately, sometimes we just may not be able to do much about the pain. However, we can begin to pay attention to the ways we resist and struggle with the pain, which can help reduce some of our suffering. Of course, this is not easy. By definition, pain hurts. We cannot will it away. But as you know, it is also not easy to keep expending so much time and energy to fight the pain. This fighting, this resistance, can be physical, mental, and emotional.

The pain itself is bad enough, but we often tend to tighten our muscles around the painful areas, usually in a subconscious attempt to "protect" them from getting worse. Ironically, that muscle tension usually grows, and spreads to more places in the body, and can create even more pain and discomfort.

Likewise, we often resist mentally and emotionally. Of course we do! No one wants to feel pain. Unfortunately, this mental resistance also can make the pain worse. It is natural for thoughts to come up about how unfair it is to be in such pain, how misunderstood you feel since no one else can "see" your pain, and how the pain is ruining your life. Of course your brain will worry about how you will be able to continue functioning with so much pain. It is also natural to feel anger, sadness, or loss because of all the problems the pain has created for you.

Unfortunately, such thoughts and emotions tend to kick up the stress response. While the stress response could save your life if you needed to fight or run away from danger, there is no one to fight or run away from in this case but your own body. What happens is that your muscles get tense, making the pain worse, and your inflammation response kicks up, which also tends to worsen the pain.

If you keep doing what you've always done, you'll keep getting what you've always gotten. Are you willing to experiment with some other ways of relating to your pain?

Let's try an exercise to explore the pain, which will begin to help you shift your relationship to it. Though you can practice this anytime and anywhere, it may be best to start in a quiet, peaceful place. Try to position yourself to be as comfortable as you can with the pain you are having. Take some deep breaths, from your belly if you can, which will help slow down the stress response. Take your time in going through the questions below. If at any point you feel like you can't continue, don't feel any pressure to keep going. Even a few seconds of exploring the pain is the beginning of developing a new relationship to it.

Where exactly are you experiencing pain right now?

_____
_____
_____

How strong is the pain in this moment, on a scale of 1-10? (1=no pain, 10= the worst possible pain you could imagine experiencing) _____

How did you arrive at that number? What information did you use to decide how much pain you are feeling? Try to be as specific as you can.

_____
_____
_____

How would you describe the physical sensations related to the pain in your body right now? Is it sharp or dull? Pulsating or steady? Is it focused in one place or spread out? It may be challenging to stay with it, but try to explore the sensations in as much detail as you can.

_____
_____
_____

Are the sensations changing from moment to moment? If so, in what ways?

_____
_____
_____

What emotions are present right now? You will likely have strong, obvious emotions, but take some time to also look for and separate out the subtler emotions that may be there.

_____

_____

_____

What thoughts are coming and going in your mind right now? Are they loud, strong, and familiar ones? Are they about the past or the future? See if you can also notice the more subtle, quiet thoughts and images in your mind.

_____

_____

_____

Some of your thoughts may be about memories from the past. What memories are coming up? Are you thinking of the ways the pain has created trouble and suffering in the past? Do you have regrets or wishes that the past could have been different?

_____

_____

_____

Are some of your thoughts about the future? Worrying about all the things that might happen, or all the problems and suffering the pain might create for you in the months or years to come?

_____

_____

_____

Now, take a few minutes to distinguish and separate out all those thoughts, memories, and emotions from the actual physical sensations in your body right now in this moment. Try not to fight with the thoughts and emotions, just keep putting your focus back into your body. Describe the physical sensations in as much detail as you can. They will probably feel worse at first, but try to continue exploring them as best you can.

_____

_____

_____

How would you rate the pain now? Did it change or stay the same?

_____

_____

_____

Many people who regularly practice the above exercise find that their resistance, and even their pain, often drops at least temporarily. However, the point is to practice staying with it, whether it drops or not, even though it is uncomfortable. If your whole life has become about avoiding the pain and discomfort, you will significantly restrict the activities in your life. You may not be able to do a lot of the things you used to do, but it doesn't mean you have to stop living.

What have you given up in your struggles with pain? What has it cost you? What people, things, or activities would you like to have more of in your life? What do you value? What is meaningful to you? What is important enough to you that you would be willing to experience some pain in order to have more of it?

_____

_____

_____

_____

_____

_____

_____

_____

_____

_____

_____

_____

_____

_____

_____

_____

THOUGHT DISORDERS

Thought disorders like schizophrenia are among the most challenging conditions a human being can experience. They can cause serious problems for clients and their families. While they can first manifest in children and in older adults, thought disorders most often begin in late adolescence or early adulthood.

Individuals with schizophrenia tend to suffer from three major symptom areas: cognitive, positive, and negative (American Psychiatric Association, 2012). Cognitive symptoms include disorganized thinking, difficulty concentrating, and memory problems. Negative symptoms involve qualities that are missing, and include apathy, restricted range of affect, and impairments in the ability to interact socially. Positive symptoms are those that are increased above what other people experience, such as racing thoughts, delusions, and hallucinations.

Tips for Working with Visions and Voices

Hallucinations are a major component of thought disorders, and can be frightening to both clients and untrained clinicians. Again, human experiences lie on a continuum. On the milder end are sensory illusions. A blurry form in the distance looks ghostly. A shadow tricks the mind into thinking something just walked past. On the more extreme end, individuals can see, hear, and interact with beings or phenomena that no one else perceives.

It is important to be sensitive to the experiences of clients, realizing that individuals with schizophrenia are doing their best to make sense of their experiences. In fact, the clinical term "hallucinations" typically has a negative connotation for clients, automatically assuming they are false, or implying that the client is "crazy." Referring to clients' experiences as "visions" and "voices" is more neutral, and sounds less judgmental, modeling for clients that they need not get caught up in struggles with their own experiences.

I once ran a psychotherapy group on an inpatient unit, and one day, a client felt safe enough to disclose that she could see angels. She nervously looked at me, worrying that I would automatically tell the psychiatrist to increase her medication. I basically said that I could certainly not judge that her experiences and perceptions were any less valid than my own. I somewhat tongue-in-cheek said that if these "angels" were ordering her to kill someone, I would be concerned, but otherwise, it was quite interesting to have such perceptions. Perhaps paradoxically, when people are no longer afraid of their visions and voices, they struggle and battle with them less, their stress levels go down, and they can spend more energy on their lives and their relationships. In fact, quite a few other group members that day felt safe to talk about their own experiences with angels, and I felt quite honored to be part of the discussion.

The practices of mindfulness and acceptance can be helpful for clients with schizophrenia, and ACT is now evidence-based for this population. The ability to decenter from our own thoughts and emotions can also help prevent people from getting lost in psychosis.

Tips for Working with Paranoia

We have all had the experience of not being believed. It can be very frustrating. Imagine that you saw a fire in the lobby of a building, and you rushed in to your office to tell everyone they needed to evacuate, but they did not believe you. You would become very adamant, because their lives would be at stake. If they kept telling you it was all in your head, you would become increasingly frustrated. However, if they went to the lobby with you, and there was no fire, only then would you calm down, and begin to think that maybe your eyes were playing tricks on you.

Likewise, directly challenging a person with clinical levels of paranoia only tends to make them worse. Once when I was on an inpatient unit at a VA hospital, a psychiatrist was interviewing a patient who was paranoid about being poisoned. The psychiatrist was carefully asking questions about who might be doing that, and how long it had been going on. One of the new medical students became impatient, and blurted out, "Why would anybody want to poison you?" The patient immediately became angry and shut down, likely suspecting the medical student was an accomplice. After all, if you were trying to poison someone, you would deny that you were doing it.

Knowing the right thing to say in the moment can be challenging before you develop experience. You do not necessarily have to join in completely with the delusions the client may be having. The main thing is to remember that at some level, what clients are perceiving "makes sense" to them, and rather than shutting them down, seek to explore and understand where they are coming from.

Using mindfulness, clients can learn to notice their symptoms early, and learn to better decenter or defuse from strong thoughts instead of automatically buying into them. They can often look back and see the path that led them to getting sick again, but usually they do not recognize the signs until it is too late.

Everyone will experience their symptoms differently, so it is helpful for clients to tune into to their own experiences, which is the aim of the following worksheet.

Paying Attention to the Signs of Your Illness

If you've been diagnosed with a thought disorder, you may have experienced someone calling you "crazy," and maybe you have even thought that yourself sometimes. But there are very real reasons for the symptoms you have experienced, just like other medical disorders. Just like diabetes is caused by an insulin imbalance, thought disorders are caused by brain chemistry imbalances. Just as diabetes can be controlled by good eating, self-care, and sometimes medicine, so it is with your illness.

The symptoms you have experienced in the past may have been quite alarming. The fear of your illness getting worse can fill you with stress and worry. While the symptoms can't always be controlled, you can learn to manage your stress, and to relate differently to your symptoms when they do start coming back. Instead of making your whole life about your illness, you can work to build a richer and more fulfilling life for yourself, even if you sometimes experience unpleasant symptoms.

You may not want to remember times when your illness created problems for you, but you may be able to learn from those experiences. Doing so will help you notice sooner if it comes back again, and you may be able to proactively prevent any symptoms from getting worse.

Reflect back on the last time your illness came on strongly. What happened? What did you experience? Who was around you? Did you notice any voices or visions?

_____

_____

_____

_____

What thoughts, feelings, body sensations, and sensory experiences did you notice during that last episode?

_____

_____

_____

_____

What were some of the earliest signs that your illness was worsening? What were some of the first thoughts to come up? What emotions were there? Were you aware of any specific body sensations? Did you notice any voices or visions?

_____

_____

_____

_____

What has been the cost of your illness? What would you like to have more of in your life? What is important to you? What are some small steps to having even a little more of that in your life, even if you sometimes will have the symptoms too?

_____

_____

_____

_____

When you notice the signs or your illness returning, what are some proactive things you can do to prevent it from getting worse? What can you do to take care of yourself? What has been helpful in the past? Who can you count on to help you through this? What professionals can support you through this? (List names and phone numbers)

_____

_____

_____

_____

Names	Phone numbers

BORDERLINE PERSONALITY DISORDER

Borderline personality disorder is characterized by signs and symptoms that include an intense fear of abandonment (real or imagined), unstable intense relationships, rapid changes in self-image, periods of paranoia and loss of contact with reality, impulsive and risky behaviors, parasuicidal behaviors, wide mood swings, feelings of emptiness, and intense anger (American Psychiatric Association, 2012).

Because these clients can be very challenging to work with, understanding this population helps the therapist develop compassion. I once overheard support staff at a mental health agency talking about a client, saying, "Her idea of monogamy is to only have sex with one person at a time." While I understand gallows humor can be a coping mechanism, the very reason that client was coming in for therapy was to get help. It can be easy to judge people by their shocking behaviors, but when we understand more about all the horrible things they went through, we can begin to help them heal and develop new ways of living in the world.

It is important to stay present with these clients, and not to fall into the trap of reacting with anger after they say or do provoking things. These individuals often have an intense history of trauma and physical and/or sexual abuse. When even their bodies were not respected as a boundary, they learned to do dramatic things to get attention or to avoid the overwhelming situations, thoughts, and feelings that come up.

Tips for Working with Dialectical Behavior Therapy

Dialectical Behavior Therapy is a well-researched, evidence-based program for working with borderline personality disorder. "Dialectics" involves balancing the extremes, since all-or-nothing, black-and-white thinking is very characteristic of this population. Clients learn to notice and work with all the shades of gray in between black and white.

DBT is best done using a team approach. A group class teaches clients the core skills of DBT. An individual therapist works with clients to manage crises and to apply the skills. An on-call therapist manages crises as they arise.

Having a dedicated on-call DBT crisis therapist interrupts the "revolving door" issue that can happen in emergency rooms and inpatient psychiatric units. If untrained, clinicians working in emergency settings might not respond well to the often times dramatic gestures they encounter from patients who have been there many times before. While these clients can be truly suicidal, their behaviors are often a result of the need to do dramatic things to manage their own emotions or to get attention. Cutting and other forms of self-mutilation can be frightening to untrained clinicians, but it is important to understand the function of the cutting, and the underlying emotional motivators. While cutting can be a serious concern, the cutting may not really be about the cutting.

There are four major modules within the DBT program, each one going into great depth with lots of examples and homework assignments for clients to practice.

- The Interpersonal Effectiveness Skills Module looks at a number of variables for becoming more skillful in relationships.
- The Emotion Regulation Skills Module explores the full range of experiencing and managing feelings.
- The Distress Tolerance Skills Module teaches clients how to survive crises and how to take care of themselves, and teaches radical acceptance skills.
- The Mindfulness Skills Module breaks down the practice of mindfulness into concrete and practical skills. It also teaches the concept of Wise Mind, which is described in the following handout.

Wise Mind

All of us have two minds: a thinking, rational mind, and an emotional, feeling mind. We can even see this in the fact that our brains are split into two hemispheres.

Sometimes we meet people who are living mostly in the rational side. They may do things that are very logical, but they seem somehow robotic. There is little life or zest in them. In science fiction shows, robots often long for the richness of human emotions.

I sometimes meet therapists or spiritual teachers who speak in a monotone, as if they are floating in another plane of existence (though in reality they may act quite differently in private settings). If your life is very chaotic and emotional, and has been for a very long time, you might think that feeling nothing would be a great thing. But we need emotions. They give richness to our lives. Emotions motivate us to take action.

Take a small, if silly, example. Once when I was about to give a presentation, I realized that I had lost the power cord to my projector. I immediately felt some anxiety. This might sound funny to say, but I *wanted* to have that anxiety. Now, I did not want to be overwhelmed by high levels of anxiety, but that little bit of anxiety told me, "Hey – this is important – you better call somebody and try to fix this." So, I talked to someone who talked to someone who called someone, and finally a technician came with the right power cord. My anxiety, which is really only energy, motivated me to do something. Had I felt no anxiety at all when the power cord was missing, I would have said to myself, "Oh well, whatever. I've already seen the presentation – I don't care about these people."

There is actually a bundle of fibers in the brain called the "corpus callosum" that connects both brain hemispheres. The goal is to be a balanced human being, making good use of both our logic and our emotions. The place where our rational minds and our emotional minds overlap is called "wise mind."

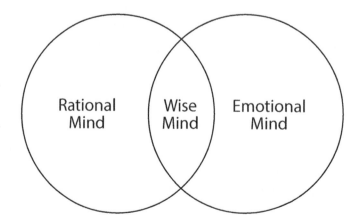

When our thoughts are racing or our emotions are raging, we get pulled away from Wise Mind, but it is always there inside of us. The first step is to practice getting in touch with it more often, before we become too intellectual or become too overwhelmed by our emotions. We often act impulsively because we cannot stand our own strong thoughts or intense emotions. But when we pause for a moment, we can remember to ask ourselves, "What would be a wise way to handle this situation?"

To reacquaint yourself with your Wise Mind, find a fairly safe and quiet place, in a peaceful room or out in nature, and keep your attention in your five senses as best you can. Notice when strong thoughts come up, but remind yourself that you don't have to argue with your own thoughts. Notice when strong feelings come up, but remember that you are more than just your feelings, and even intense emotions will pass, just as no storm lasts forever.

When you first practice, you may only get a fleeting glimpse of your Wise Mind, but over time, you will be able to get there more easily and more often. You cannot always control your thoughts or your emotions, but you can control what you choose to do. If you first seek to get in touch with that balanced Wise Mind, you are more likely to take wise actions, even if your thoughts and feelings sometimes play their old negative, habitual recordings.

CHAIN ANALYSIS

Individuals with borderline personality disorder have often lived through a long string of horrible and even abusive experiences in the past. Unfortunately, the skills they used to survive abusive situations, such as mistrusting people and doing dramatic things to get attention, create problems in their current daily lives and relationships, in a sort of self-fulfilling prophecy. Clients tend to feel hopeless that they are constantly being tossed around by the whims of bad luck. They may not even be aware of their own contributions to current life situations. Clients are taught that they can only control their own behaviors, not anyone else's.

In the DBT skills training program, clients practice chain analysis to better understand why they engage in behaviors that create problems for them. The handout may be helpful for any client who feels that they are having trouble controlling their own behaviors.

Analyzing the Chain of Events that Led to a Problem Behavior

Have you ever found yourself doing something you later regretted, like saying something harsh to someone, hurting yourself, or going back to an addiction? Maybe you told yourself you would never do it again, or maybe you felt like someone else drove you to do it. It's so easy to blame everyone else for why we do things, or why we react the way we do. You probably have every right to do so, since you may experience terrible mistreatment in your life.

However, if you always blame others, or your situation, this means your life and happiness is completely based on what others do, or on the random events in the environment. That's a hell of a way to live.

When you begin to pay attention, you will notice that every situation has a number of causes and conditions. Instead of feeling like we are subject to the whims of others, or that we are helpless puppets of a cruel universe, we can start to notice and alter the causes before they lead to future problems.

Of course, if others treated us better, or could read our minds, or the universe would just pay us back in a positive way for all the crap we have endured, all would be well. It sure would be great if that happened, but we really cannot control those variables. The only things we can control are our own actions.

Use this worksheet any time you have done something you later regretted. By paying attention to the causes and conditions that led to the behavior, you might notice some connections that will help you prevent it in the future.

What exactly is the problem behavior that you want to analyze?

_____

_____

_____

What was the prompting or triggering event? What was going on around you that got the problem behavior started? When did it get started?

_____

_____

_____

What made you vulnerable to this behavior getting started? What was going on inside you or around you that made you more susceptible to doing the problem behavior?

_____

_____

_____

What were the consequences of engaging in the problem behavior, in the environment as well as in yourself? What harm did this problem behavior cause?

_____

_____

_____

In the left-hand column, in as much detail as you can, list the links in the chain of events that led from the vulnerability and the situation to the problem behavior. Include actions, body sensations, thoughts, feelings, and events in the environment. Then, go back and fill out the right-hand column with more skillful behaviors you could have used to break the chain that led to the problem behavior. You can start with the columns below, and continue on a separate sheet of paper.

Chain of Events	Skillful Behaviors

What steps can you take to prevent this problem behavior in the future? What can you do to reduce your vulnerability? What can you do to prevent the prompting or triggering event from happening, or at least from triggering you?

_____

_____

_____

You cannot go back in time to undo the problem behavior you did, but is there anything you can do now or in the near future to repair or correct any harm you did to others or yourself?

_____

_____

_____

NEUROCOGNITIVE DISORDERS

Mindfulness can also be helpful for older individuals, as well as for the people who care for them. Retirement can often bring up questions about the meaning and purpose of life, and can trigger anxiety or depression about the inevitable approach of death. Declining memory and physical health is a continuous reminder of the impermanence of things.

Mindfulness can be a tool to practice flowing with these challenges, and to not get so caught up in battling with them. It can also allow people, perhaps even for the first time in their lives, to realize they are not merely living to "get somewhere," but can enjoy each moment for what it is.

While significant cognitive decline is not inevitable with aging, the older one gets, the higher the chances of succumbing to such problems. Dementia, now known as neurocognitive disorder, is a brain-based degenerative process due to disease, stroke, or trauma that results in memory and other cognitive problems (American Psychiatric Association, 2012). Alzheimer's disease, one of the most common types, develops as a result of tangles and plaques forming in the brain, interfering with the functioning of the neurons and their connections. It begins with minor memory problems, like word-finding difficulties, and eventually leads to death when it disrupts the life-support functions of the brain.

Programs such as Mindfulness-Based Elder Care (MBEC: McBee, 2008) appear promising to older adults in the early stages of dementia. Clients often experience frustration about their declining memory, which tends to interfere with memory. The MBEC program operates as if each session is the only one, though it may highlight different exercises in different sessions. Clients are not expected to remember complicated instructions. Though a key ingredient in all mindfulness programs, it is especially important with this population for the therapist to model and provide an atmosphere of acceptance of even difficult thoughts and emotions. The MBEC protocol also recommends engaging the clients' senses to bring them into the present moment, through such things as music, smells, and light massage.

Family members and professional caregivers can be especially prone to develop stress-related problems when caring for older adults with dementia. The next worksheet may be helpful for caregivers to understand the challenges involved in caring for a loved one with a progressive neurocognitive disorder.

When a Loved One Has Dementia

Watching a loved one gradually lose their faculties can be a very painful experience. In the early stages, many people do not even realize how bad things are getting. Understanding what is happening can be helpful to reduce the frustration that may come up for you.

In the early stages of a disease like Alzheimer's, the person has trouble remembering minor things like names or where they left their keys or glasses. As the disease spreads through the brain, it becomes more and more difficult to remember things, but they may still have their social skills intact to cover up their deficits. They might say something like, "Now, it's not polite to ask how old someone is," but in fact they do not remember their own age. They may even appear to maintain conversations, but most of what they say is very generic.

Many people with dementia experience "sundowning." They might seem more like themselves in the morning, but they get worse as the day goes on, and have the most trouble by the time the sun goes down.

Over time, the disease spreads more and more throughout the brain, affecting more of their abilities. Spatial perception begins to worsen, making it difficult to get around. They may get lost when walking familiar routes, and may start bumping into things. Even though memory continues to get worse, they may still recall childhood memories well, because those old memories have been stored all throughout the brain. They may eventually think that you are an old childhood friend, because they can feel that they love you, but they only have access to older memories.

When your loved one forgets your name, or mixes up "he" and "she," there is no need to correct them. Doing so only creates frustration for both of you. If they say they need clothes, and you just went shopping, don't say, "Don't you remember what we did yesterday?" Just say, "You got some new clothes in your closet now. What would you like to wear today?"

It helps to just meet your loved one where they are in that moment. Having dementia is like being in a dream. Have you ever had a strange dream that kept shifting? Maybe one moment you were driving a car, then the next moment you were flying a spaceship, then the next moment you were talking to a celebrity. When you woke up, you realized that the dream was made up of completely disconnected situations and made no sense, but when you were in the dream, you were only in each moment of it, and were doing what made sense in that moment.

It is the same with a person who has dementia. They begin to lose the sense of things being connected, and are just in each moment. If they find themselves in front of a door, since doors are for opening and going through, they may go out the door without even knowing why. Just covering doorknobs with long curtains drastically cuts the frequency of wandering behavior.

If you can learn to meet your loved one in each moment, you will both be less frustrated and enjoy each other's company more. Remember too that your attitude, tone, and presence will likely be more important than any words you say.

Most importantly, remember to take care of yourself. It is very common to become overly focused on taking care of your loved one, and to neglect yourself. You will be grieving, and it can be even more complicated than if they had died, because they are only dying a little bit at a time. In rare moments, your loved one may seem more like themselves again, which makes it all the more difficult when they become lost again.

Take some time to work through the questions below. Putting your thoughts down on paper can give you some perspective on them.

First of all, write down what you have been experiencing, and what has been most difficult so far.

_____

_____

Do you find yourself thinking a lot about the past? What memories come up for you? How well do you remember the good times? Do you have any regrets?

_____

_____

What are your biggest fears and concerns about the future?

_____

_____

What thoughts, feelings, and body sensations are coming up for you as you are filling this out? Do they come up a lot when you think of your loved one? Are you willing to just let the thoughts and feelings be here while you make your choices about how best to help your loved one?

_____

_____

What simple things can you do to take care of yourself? Think both short term, when you feel distressed, and long term, to keep your overall stress levels down. Are there any hobbies, activities, or relationships that you have cut back on or given up? Are you getting enough sleep, eating well, and engaging in physical activities or exercise?

_____

_____

Not everyone will understand what you are going through. Who can you look to for social support during this process? Consider close friends, family members, therapists, and organizations like your local Alzheimer's Association.

_____

_____

Part 7

Tools for Diversity, Social Justice and Mindfulness

Since mindfulness is about paying attention, and about noticing reality as it is whether we like it or not, it can be an important tool for addressing diversity and social justice issues. Increasingly, studies are being done with mindfulness to improve diversity awareness and to reduce discrimination (Berila, 2014; Masuda, 2014).

A recent study by the American Psychological Association (2016) found that 69% of individuals in the United States have experienced discrimination, with 61% experiencing it on a day-to-day basis, such as being treated with less courtesy or respect, and/or being threatened or harassed. The study also found that discrimination has a significant impact on stress and health.

CULTURAL COMPETENCE

It is crucial to be aware of diversity issues in order to be a competent clinician. State boards are increasingly reprimanding clinicians for working with cultural groups with whom they have not been trained to work. In my state, whenever I renew my psychology license, I receive a list of others who have lost their licenses or have received reprimands. It is not unusual to see someone reprimanded for working with a population or cultural group they were not trained to work with.

When I was in graduate school, I completed a wonderful nine-month program on mental health and Deafness, run by Dr. Bob Basil and his colleagues. Half of the participants were clinicians, and we were able to learn about Deaf culture and the important considerations for doing therapy with this population. The other participants were sign language interpreter students, who learned about the issues and nuances of interpreting in a mental health setting. The program consisted of biweekly didactic sessions on topics related to Deafness and mental health. We also had a weekly clinic in which we conducted psychotherapy and psychological assessments with Deaf individuals under the guidance of our supervisors.

The program was very enlightening, and I cannot imagine doing work with this population without such training. I cringe when I see an email on a listserv from someone asking about getting a sign language interpreter when they have no experience with Deaf culture. I understand that if they are the only provider in the area, they may have to do the best they can, but they at least need to seek out training, consultation, or supervision, or they could cause the client harm. For example, if you don't know that sign language uses strong gestures and facial expressions in place of vocal tone, you might think the client is emotionally labile when they tell a vivid story and then go back to neutral affect. If you don't know that another convention is to spell people's names only once then "place" them in the air, and then to point to or interact with that space in the air when referencing a person, you might think the client is talking to imaginary people in the sky or hallucinating.

Of course, becoming more culturally competent does not mean stereotyping, which involves making automatic assumptions about the person or population with whom you are working. Do not fall into the trap of thinking, "because this person is _____, then she must be _____."

Training in diversity helps us keep potential working hypotheses in mind, so we do not accidentally miss important aspects of clients and their values and experiences. In fact, "cultural humility" may be a more useful term, since we can never fully know everything about a particular population, and especially not about the particular individual in front of us (Gallardo, 2014). Cultural humility requires a great deal of self-awareness on the part of the clinician.

SELF-AWARENESS

Self-awareness is a very important component of cultural competency. When I first attended graduate school, the program boasted that the entire curriculum emphasized cultural diversity, with nine required classes specifically on this topic. At the time, I assumed that since I was a nice person, had travelled to some other parts of the world, and had studied several languages, I probably did not need that training. As I went through the coursework, I became increasing aware of how very naïve I had been. I had no idea how little awareness I really had of these issues, and of the unconscious biases I had programmed into me by society, and of the privileges that I took for granted.

When I was a practicum student, I remember sitting down for my final evaluation with one of my supervisors, who happened to be an older white male. When we got to the section on diversity, he looked up at me and said, "You treat everyone the same, so I will give you a high mark on that."

I would guess that supervisor meant I did not treat people who were different from me unfairly. Unfortunately, treating everyone the same in psychotherapy is bad practice. People are different, and have different values and life experiences. Since I am a white male, treating everyone the same would probably mean treating them all as if they were white males, which they are certainly not. We need to have awareness of how people are different in order to respect those differences. As a white male, I have experienced certain privileges in this society, and I have not experienced the same degree of discrimination as other groups have. For example, since I am heterosexual, I have no problem expressing affection toward my partner in public. However, if I push a client to come out of the closet when they are hesitant and unprepared for the consequences, I could cause them harm, if not death. Though it is absolutely unfair and illegal, people are still being mistreated and even murdered because of their sexual orientation, so we must be cautious not to push our own unexamined assumptions on others.

CLIENT-CENTERED LANGUAGE

It is especially important to pay attention to how you refer to your clients. None of us want to be primarily identified with a diagnosis. If you walked into your physician's office, and the receptionist, nurse, and physician all referred to you simply as "the diabetic," you would likely feel rather dismissed. If you have diabetes, you are still a human being with many other issues than just the regulation of your blood sugar levels. In fact, your visit that day to the doctor might have nothing at all to do with your diabetes.

Likewise, watch out for referring to clients as "the borderline" or "the schizophrenic." It may seem bulky if you are not used to it, but it is important to say "my client with borderline personality disorder" or "the individual with schizophrenia." Whether or not clients can hear you, this language reminds everyone (including yourself) that you are working with a human being first, who happens to have issues that need to be addressed. This is especially true for clients, since they can easily become overly identified with a diagnosis, and they likely already feel ostracized from others in society. Likewise, tactfully correcting colleagues and peers reminds them that they are working with human beings who have feelings just like everyone else. Labeling clients as a diagnosis is a form of microaggression.

MICROAGGRESSIONS

Microaggressions are slights, put-downs, or behaviors with a connotation expressing sexism, racism, heterosexism, ableism, etc.

While the word "micro" technically means small, microaggressions may feel huge to the person receiving them. The person doing it may not have any awareness that they are doing it, and probably would never consciously intend to do it, but the impact on the person receiving it is very real, though the receiver may question themselves about it.

Not long ago, I co-edited a book with a female colleague (Sears & Niblick, 2014), and the publisher sent us both an email. The email began with, "Dear Dr. Sears and Alison". Alison in fact has a doctorate degree also. While I do not mind whether or not I am called doctor, calling a man doctor and a woman with a doctorate degree by her first name is definitely a microaggression. I have to confess that many years ago, I might not have even noticed such a thing, or I might have quickly dismissed it as no big deal. However, I try to pay attention, and I have noticed times when I am in a room full of individuals with doctorate degrees, and the men are preferentially addressed as "Dr.," while the women are more likely to be addressed by their first names. This sends a strong message to the women that they are not as valued or respected.

After bringing the biased nature of the email we received to the attention of the publisher, I also sent an email to Dr. Niblick (Alison). I basically apologized for the blatant sexism of the way the email addressed her. She wrote me back and thanked me for bringing that up so directly. She said she had felt awkward about the email for some reason, but could not put her finger on exactly why until I had sent her my email. She realized that the way it had been worded made her feel like a less valued member of the team, even though she had worked very hard on the project.

Chances are, clients will not say to you, "I'm sure you're doing this unconsciously, but I'm feeling somehow slighted based on my background characteristics." They will probably just feel uncomfortable and disappear. Clients are often forgiving when we make sincere efforts to be aware of issues of social justice and diversity, but it is not their job to educate us. The onus is on us to make the effort to stay up to date through research and consultation. We also need to have the courage to honestly look at ourselves, and to receive open feedback from trusted colleagues.

SOCIAL JUSTICE ISSUES

Social justice involves fair access to and distribution of power, resources, and opportunities within society. Despite the ideals of modern society, major inequities still exist in our culture. In addition to awareness of these issues, therapists can leverage their own power and privilege through advocacy efforts. In our clinical work, this may involve addressing such things as access to therapy, cost and frequency of sessions, and resources available to clients. Many professional associations ask therapists to do pro bono work, give "scholarships" to clients who need them, and/or get involved in their communities.

We cannot expect those who are being oppressed to overcome the oppression on their own. When those of us in a position of power and privilege, as educated therapists are, witness injustices, like microaggressions, we need to speak up, or at least indicate in some way that we are not okay with such things. When we do nothing, the injustices in our society will be perpetuated.

These issues often come up in therapy sessions. If a client says something blatantly sexist, for example, and you ignore it, you are implying that such attitudes are okay. However, it is important to be skillful in how you address it. If you yell at a brand new client with, "You sexist pig!", it will not help anything. The client will get angry and quit, thinking you are a "crazy feminist." However, even a facial cringe shows the client you are not in agreement. As rapport deepens, you might inquire about how such attitudes have impacted the client's relationships.

A couple of times, in my organizational consulting work, I became aware of significant diversity issues, even though I was not hired to attend to them. However, I at least felt an obligation to bring this up skillfully with leadership, saying something like, "I know you asked me to consult on XYZ, but I couldn't help noticing another situation going on in your organization, which if not addressed immediately, could get you into some very serious legal trouble. Would you like to discuss that?"

Diversity and social justice issues can be uncomfortable to openly talk about, and can certainly bring up a lot of emotions for people. However, it is crucial to continue the dialogues and the work, even if we make embarrassing mistakes from time to time. There are still things like race riots happening around the world, inequities in pay for men and women, and people being murdered based on their religion or skin color. If we cannot address these topics as mental health professionals, what hope is there for the future of humankind?

The following two worksheets are designed for mental health professionals and students to increase their awareness of and sensitivity to issues of diversity.

Diversity
Awareness Inventory

Diversity awareness is an important component of being a culturally competent clinician. Use this worksheet to reflect on your own aspects of diversity, and on your competence to work with diverse clients. Ideally, take some time to ponder these questions in depth, rather than answering quickly and superficially.

An important factor in cultural competence is self-awareness. Sometimes we are too close to see things, or take our values and viewpoints for granted. Take some time to reflect on and write about your own aspects of diversity. Include the ways you identify with and relate to your gender, race/culture, sexual orientation, physical ability, spirituality, socio-economic status, etc.

_____

_____

In what ways have you experienced discrimination in the past for any of those aspects of yourself?

_____

_____

Do you currently experience discrimination? How does it manifest?

_____

_____

In what ways have you experienced power and privilege in the past? (Opportunities, resources, or influence that others in this society do not necessarily have)

_____

_____

In what areas do you currently have at least some degree of power or privilege?

_____

_____

In addition to self-awareness, it is important to receive training in the clinical issues of working with diverse populations. Take some time to reflect on your past training and on needed areas for improvement. Consider all the ways you have been trained and could receive future training, such as workshops, classes, books, consultation, and supervision.

Under each topic, jot down your areas of strength and areas for improvement in terms of your knowledge and ability to work with each population:

Gender issues:

_____

_____

Spirituality and religion:

_____

_____

Sexual orientation:

_____

_____

Race/culture:

_____

_____

Ability status:

_____

_____

Socio-economic status:

_____

_____

Other areas of diversity:

_____

_____

Getting honest, objective feedback is very important. With whom can you openly discuss these topics? (colleagues, supervisors, friends)

_____

_____

_____

_____

_____

Reflecting on Microaggressions

Microaggressions are slights, put-downs, or behaviors that have a sexist, racist, heterosexist, ableist, etc. tone. While the word "micro" technically means small, microaggressions may not feel small to the person receiving them. The person doing it may not have any awareness that they are doing it, and probably would never consciously intend to do it, but the impact on the person receiving it is very real, though they may question themselves about it.

In order to better understand and prevent microaggressions in your own life and clinical practice, it can be helpful to reflect on your previous experiences.

What microaggressions have you personally experienced? Because they were probably uncomfortable experiences, they may not easily come to mind, so take some time to carefully reflect. Think back as far as you can remember, as long ago as early childhood. Consider also any very recent experiences.

_____

_____

_____

How did those microaggressions affect you emotionally?

_____

_____

_____

What things did you do when you experienced microaggressions?

_____

_____

_____

Looking back on it, what would you have done differently, if anything?

_____

_____

_____

What microaggressions have you witnessed being done to others? Again, it may be challenging to remember them, since they will be uncomfortable.

_____

_____

_____

What impact did it have on the person receiving it?

_____

_____

_____

What do you wish you would have done or said differently at the time, if given the opportunity?

_____

_____

_____

What microaggressions have you yourself committed in the past?

_____

_____

_____

What impact do you think they may have had on the people receiving them?

_____

_____

_____

What would you have done or said differently, if you could go back in time?

_____

_____

_____

Of all the things you've been reflecting on above, what have you learned? How can you apply your insights into your current and future clinical work, and perhaps even in your personal life? Can you constructively repair any past hurts you may have caused?

_____

_____

_____

What has it been like to fill out this worksheet? This topic can bring up very uncomfortable feelings. This is not necessarily a bad thing, as it can help us have more empathy for others in the future. But if you're feeling overwhelmed, how can you take care of yourself? Who can you process this with?

_____

_____

_____

Resources

Suggested CBT and Mindfulness Resources

BOOKS FOR CLIENTS

Dahl, J. A., & Lundgren, T. (2006). *Living beyond your pain: Using acceptance and commitment therapy to ease chronic pain*. Oakland, CA: New Harbinger Publications.

Davis, L. (2016). *Meditations for Healing Trauma: Mindfulness Skills to Relieve Post-Traumatic Stress*. Oakland, CA: New Harbinger.

Greenberger, D., & Padesky, C. A. (2015). *Mind over mood: Change how you feel by changing the way you think* (2nd ed.). New York: Guilford Press.

Harris, R. (2009). *ACT with love: Stop struggling, reconcile differences, and strengthen your relationship with acceptance and commitment therapy*. Oakland, CA: New Harbinger.

Hayes, S. C., & Smith, S. (2005). *Get out of your mind and into your life*. Oakland, CA: New Harbinger.

Kristeller, J., & Bowman, A. (2015). *The joy of half a cookie: Using mindfulness to lose weight and end the struggle with food*. New York: Perigee.

McGrath, P. B. (2007). *The OCD answer book: Professional answers to more than 250 top questions about obsessive-compulsive disorder*. Naperville, IL: Sourcebooks.

Sears, R. (2014). *Mindfulness: Living through challenges and enriching your life in this moment*. London, UK: Wiley-Blackwell.

Teasdale, J., Williams, M., & Segal, Z. (2014). *The mindful way workbook: An 8-week program to free yourself from depression and emotional distress*. New York: Guilford Press.

Walser, R. D., & Westrup, D. (2009). *The mindful couple: How acceptance and mindfulness can lead you to the love you want*. Oakland, CA: New Harbinger Publications.

Williams, M., & Penman, D. (2011). *Mindfulness: An eight-week plan for finding peace in a frantic world*. Emmaus, PA: Rodale Books.

Williams, M., Teasdale, J., Segal, Z., & Kabat-Zinn, J. (2007). *The mindful way through depression: Freeing yourself from chronic unhappiness*. New York: Guilford Press.

CBT BOOKS

Barkley, R. A. (1997). *Defiant children: A clinician's manual for assessment and parent training* (2nd ed.). New York: Guilford Press.

Ciarrochi, J., & Bailey, A. (2009). *A CBT-practitioner's guide to ACT: How to bridge the gap between cognitive behavioral therapy and acceptance and commitment therapy.* Oakland, CA: New Harbinger.

Ellis, A., & Harper, R. A. (1975). *A new guide to rational living.* Englewood Cliffs, NJ: Prentice-Hall.

Eyberg, S. M., & Funderburk, B. (2011). *PCIT: Parent-child interaction therapy protocol.* Gainesville, FL: PCIT International, Inc.

Friedberg, R. D., McClure, J. M., & Garcia, J. H. (2009). *Cognitive therapy techniques for children and adolescents: Tools for enhancing practice.* New York: Guilford Press.

Hofmann, S. G., Dozois, D. J. A., Rief, W., & Smits, J. A. J. (2014). *The Wiley handbook of cognitive behavioral therapy.* London, UK: Wiley-Blackwell.

Leahy, R. (2003). *Cognitive therapy techniques: A practitioner's guide.* New York: Guilford Press.

Leahy, R. L. (2003). *Roadblocks in cognitive-behavioral therapy: Transforming challenges into opportunities for change.* New York: Guilford Press.

McMullin, R. (2000). *The new handbook of cognitive therapy techniques* (rev. ed.). New York: W.W. Norton.

Monson, C. M., & Fredman, S. J. (2012). *Cognitive-behavioral conjoint therapy for PTSD: Harnessing the healing power of relationships.* New York: Guilford Press.

Riggenbach, J. (2013). *The CBT Toolbox: A Workbook for Clients and Clinicians.* Eau Claire, WI: PESI Publishing & Media, Inc.

MBCT BOOKS AND ARTICLES

Bartley, T. (2011). *Mindfulness-based cognitive therapy for cancer.* London, UK: Wiley-Blackwell.

Bowen, S., Chawla, N., & Marlatt, A. (2010). *Mindfulness-based relapse prevention for addictive behaviors: A clinician's guide.* New York: Guilford Press.

Collard, P. (2013). *Mindfulness-based cognitive therapy for dummies.* Chichester, West Sussex, UK: John Wiley & Sons.

Crane, R. (2009). *Mindfulness-based cognitive therapy.* London and New York: Routledge.

Crane, R., Kuyken, W., Williams, M., Hastings, R., Cooper, L., & Fennell, M. (2012). Competence in teaching mindfulness-based courses: Concepts, development, and assessment. *Mindfulness, 3,* 76-84. Doi: 0.1007/s12671-011-0073-2.

Deckersbach, T., Hölzel, B., Eisner, L., Lazar, S., & Nierenberg, A. (2014). *Mindfulness-based cognitive therapy for bipolar disorder.* New York: Guilford Press.

Sears, R. (2015). *Building competence in mindfulness-based cognitive therapy: Transcripts and insights for working with stress, anxiety, depression, and other problems*. New York: Routledge.

Sears, R., & Chard, K. (2016). *Mindfulness-based cognitive therapy for PTSD*. London, UK: Wiley-Blackwell.

Segal, Z., Teasdale, J., Williams, M., & Gemar, M. (2002). The mindfulness-based cognitive therapy adherence scale: Inter-rater reliability, adherence to protocol and treatment distinctiveness. *Clinical Psychology & Psychotherapy, 9*(2), 131–138. doi: 10.1002/cpp.320.

Segal, Z., Williams, M., & Teasdale, J. (2013). *Mindfulness-based cognitive therapy for depression* (2nd ed.). New York: Guilford Press.

Semple, R., & Lee, J. (2011). *Mindfulness-based cognitive therapy for anxious children*. Oakland, CA: New Harbinger Publications, Inc.

Woods, S. (2013). Building a framework for mindful inquiry. *www.slwoods.com*

OTHER MINDFULNESS-RELATED BOOKS AND ARTICLES

Albers, S. (2003). *Eating mindfully: How to end mindless eating and enjoy a balanced relationship with food*. Oakland, CA: New Harbinger Publications, Inc.

Bogels, S., & Restifo, K. (2014). *Mindful parenting: A guide for mental health practitioners*. New York: Springer.

Carson, J. W., Carson, K. M., Gil, K. M., & Baucom, D. H. (2004). Mindfulness-based relationship enhancement. *Behavior therapy, 35*(3), 471-494.

Didonna, F. (Ed.) (2009). *Clinical handbook of mindfulness*. New York: Springer.

Duncan, L., & Bardacke, N. (2010). Mindfulness-based childbirth and parenting education: Promoting family mindfulness during the perinatal period. *Journal of Child & Family Studies, 19*, 190–202. DOI 10.1007/s10826-009-9313-7.

Hanson, R., & Mendius, R. (2009). *Buddha's brain: The practical neuroscience of happiness, love & wisdom*. Oakland, CA: New Harbinger Publications.

Follette, V. M., Briere, J., Rozelle, D., Hopper, J. W., & Rome, D. I. (Eds.) (2015). *Mindfulness-oriented interventions for trauma: Integrating contemplative practices*. New York: The Guilford Press.

Fulton, P. (2005). Mindfulness as clinical training. In C. Germer, R. Siegel, & P. Fulton (Eds.), *Mindfulness and psychotherapy*. New York: Guilford Press.

Gunaratana, H. (2011). *Mindfulness in plain English*. Boston, MA: Wisdom Publications.

Hayes, S. C, Strosahl, K., & Wilson, K. G. (2012). *Acceptance and commitment therapy: The process and practice of mindful change*. New York: Guilford Press.

Hölzel, B., Lazar, S., Gard, T., Schuman-Olivier, Z., Vago, D., & Ott, U. (2011). How does mindfulness meditation work? Proposing mechanisms of action from a conceptual and neural perspective. *Perspectives on Psychological Science, 6* (6) 537-559. DOI: 10.1177/1745691611419671.

Isis, P. (2016). *The mindful doodle book: 75 creative exercises to help you live in the moment.* Eau Claire, WI: PESI Publishing & Media.

Jacobs, A. M., Hopton, J., Davies, D., Wright, N. P., Kelly, O. P., & Turkington, D. (2014). *Treating Psychosis: A Clinician's Guide to Integrating Acceptance and Commitment Therapy, Compassion-Focused Therapy, and Mindfulness Approaches within the Cognitive Behavioral Therapy Tradition.* Oakland, CA: New Harbinger Publications.

Kabat-Zinn, J. (2013). *Full catastrophe living: Using the wisdom of your body and mind to face stress, pain, and illness* (rev. ed.). New York: Bantam.

Kabat-Zinn, J. (2006). *Coming to our senses: Healing ourselves and the world through mindfulness.* New York: Hyperion.

Kabat-Zinn, J. (1994). *Wherever you go there you are.* New York: Hyperion.

Kristeller, J., Baer, R., & Quillian, R. (2006). Mindfulness-based approaches to eating disorders. In R. A. Baer (Ed.), *Mindfulness and acceptance-based interventions: Conceptualization, application, and empirical support.* San Diego, CA: Elsevier, 75-91.

Kristeller, J., & Wolever, R. (2011). Mindfulness-based eating awareness training for treating binge eating disorder: The conceptual foundation. *Eating Disorders, 19*(1), 49-61. DOI: 10.1080/10640266.2011.533605.

Linehan, M. (2015a). *DBT skills training handouts and worksheets.* New York: Guilford Press.

Linehan, M. (2015b). *Skills training manual for treating borderline personality disorder (2nd ed.).* New York: Guilford Press.

Luedtke, B., Davis, L., & Monson, C. (2015). Mindfulness-based cognitive-behavioral conjoint therapy for posttraumatic stress disorder: a case study. *Journal of Contemporary Psychotherapy, 45*(4), 227-234. doi:10.1007/s10879-015-9298-z.

McBee, L. (2008). *Mindfulness-based elder care: A CAM model for frail elders and their caregivers.* New York: Springer Pub.

McCown, D., Reibel, D., & Micozzi, M. (2011). *Teaching mindfulness: A practical guide for clinicians and educators.* New York: Springer.

Masuda, A. (2014). *Mindfulness and acceptance in multicultural competency: A contextual approach to sociocultural diversity in theory and practice.* Oakland: New Harbinger Publications.

Morris, E. M. J., Johns, L. C., & Oliver, J. E. (Eds.) (2013). *Acceptance and Commitment Therapy and Mindfulness for Psychosis.* Hoboken, NJ: Wiley.

Niemiec, R. (2014). *Mindfulness and character strengths: A practical guide to flourishing.* Boston, MA: Hogrefe Publishing.

Pederson, L. (2015). *Dialectical behavior therapy: A contemporary guide for practitioners.* Chichester, West Sussex, UK: Wiley-Blackwell.

Santorelli, S. (2000). *Heal thy self: Lessons on mindfulness in medicine.* New York: Crown Publishers.

Sears, R., Tirch, D., & Denton, R. (2011). *Mindfulness in clinical practice.* Sarasota, FL: Professional Resource Press.

Siegel, D. (2007). *The mindful brain: Reflection and attunement in the cultivation of well-being.* New York: W. W. Norton & Company.

Walser, R. D., & Westrup, D. (2007). *Acceptance & commitment therapy for the treatment of post-traumatic stress disorder & trauma-related problems: A practitioner's guide to using mindfulness & acceptance strategies.* Oakland, CA: New Harbinger.

OTHER RELEVANT CLINICAL BOOKS

Cohen, J. A., Mannarino, A. P., & Deblinger, E. (2006). *Treating trauma and traumatic grief in children and adolescents.* New York: The Guilford Press.

Corey, G. (2012). *Theory & practice of group counseling* (8th ed.). Belmont, CA: Brooks/Cole, Cengage Learning.

Fouad, N., Gerstein, L., & Toporek, R. (2006). Social justice and counseling psychology in context. In R. Toporek, L. Gerstein, N. Fouad, G. Roysircar, & T. Israel (Eds.), *Handbook for social justice in counseling psychology.* Thousand Oaks, CA: Sage Publications.

Miller, W., & Rollnick, S. (2013). *Motivational interviewing: Helping people change* (3rd ed.). New York, NY: Guilford Press.

Ponterotto, J., Casas, J., Suzuki, L., & Alexander, C. (2010). *Handbook of multicultural counseling* (3rd ed.). Los Angeles, CA: SAGE Publications.

Sears, R. (2017). *The sense of self: Perspectives from science and Zen Buddhism.* London, UK: Palgrave MacMillan.

Sears, R., & Niblick, A. (Eds.) (2014). *Perspectives on spirituality and religion in psychotherapy.* Sarasota, FL: Professional Resource Press.

Sears, R., Rudisill, J., & Mason-Sears, C. (2006). *Consultation skills for mental health professionals.* New York: John Wiley & Sons.

Sue, D. W. (2010). *Microaggressions in everyday life: Race, gender, and sexual orientation.* Hoboken, NJ: Wiley.

Sue, D. W., & Sue, D. (2016). *Counseling the culturally diverse: Theory and practice.* Hoboken, NJ: John Wiley & Sons, Inc.

Yalom, I., & Leszcz, M. (2005). *The theory and practice of group psychotherapy* (5th ed.). New York: Basic Books.

AUDIO AND VIDEO WORKSHOPS

Kabat-Zinn, J., & Moyers, B. (1993). *Healing from within* [video]. New York: Ambrose Video. Episode of the Bill Moyers series, *Healing and the Mind*, that follows Jon Kabat-Zinn taking a group through the eight weeks of an MBSR course.

Sears, R. (2016). *Mindfulness-Based Cognitive Therapy* [video file]. Eau Claire, WI: PESI Inc. *http://www.pesi.com/store/detail/16285/mindfulness-based-cognitive-therapy-mbct*. Twelve-hour CE video workshop.

Segal, Z. (2008). *Mindfulness-based Cognitive Therapy for Depression and Anxiety* [CD]. Lancaster, PA: J&K Seminars, LLC. Two-day MBCT workshop on audio.

Segal, Z., & Carlson, J. (2005). *Mindfulness-based cognitive therapy for depression* [DVD]. Washington, DC: American Psychological Association. *http://www.apa.org/pubs/videos/4310714. aspx*. DVD video of Zindel Segal conducting the first session of MBCT, with an interview with Jon Carlson.

Williams, M. (2009). *Mindfulness-based cognitive therapy and the prevention of depression: Training video*. New York, NY: Association for Behavioral and Cognitive Therapies. DVD video of Mark Williams covering basic principles of MBCT.

MINDFULNESS EXERCISE AUDIO RECORDINGS

Purchasers of the two books below are given a website for free downloads of mindfulness exercises they can share with clients:

Segal, Z., Williams, M., & Teasdale, J. (2013). *Mindfulness-based cognitive therapy for depression* (2nd ed.). New York: Guilford Press.

Teasdale, J., Williams, M., & Segal, Z. (2014). *The mindful way workbook: An 8-week program to free yourself from depression and emotional distress*. New York: Guilford Press.

The book below comes with an audio CD of mindfulness exercises recorded by Jon Kabat-Zinn: Williams, M., Teasdale, J., Segal, Z., & Kabat-Zinn, J. (2007). *The mindful way through depression: Freeing yourself from chronic unhappiness*. New York: Guilford Press.

Jon Kabat-Zinn's mindfulness audio recordings *www.mindfulnesscds.com*

Kabat-Zinn, J. (2006). *Mindfulness for beginners* [audio CD]. Louisville, CO: Sounds True.

Kabat-Zinn, J. (2010). *Mindfulness meditation for pain relief: Guided practices for reclaiming your body and your life* [audio CD]. Boulder, CO: Sounds True.

Richard Sears (author's website) *www.psych-insights.com/mindfulness*

Sears, R. W., Tirch, D. D., & Denton, R. B. (2011). *Mindfulness practices* [audio CD]. Sarasota, FL: Professional Resource Press.

Woods, S. (2010). *Mindfulness meditation with Susan Woods* [audio CD]. Stowe, VT: Author.

SELECTED WEBSITES

Acceptance and Commitment Therapy
http://contextualscience.org

Association for Behavioral and Cognitive Therapies
http://www.abct.org

The Center for Mindfulness in Medicine, Health Care, and Society, University of Massachusetts Medical School
www.umassmed.edu/cfm

The Centre for Mindfulness Studies in Toronto
http://www.mindfulnessstudies.com

Couple Therapy for PTSD
http://www.coupletherapyforptsd.com/

Cognitive Processing Therapy (Author's Website)
http://cptforptsd.com

Cognitive Processing Therapy Online Training (CPT Web)
https://cpt.musc.edu/

Dialectical Behavior Therapy
http://behavioraltech.org

The International Society for Traumatic Stress Studies
http://www.istss.org

Mindful Awareness Research Center
marc.ucla.edu

Mindfulness-based cognitive therapy
www.mbct.com

Mindfulness Research Guide
www.mindfulexperience.org

Mindfulness-Based Relapse Prevention for Addictive Behaviors
www.mindfulrp.com

National Center for PTSD, U.S. Department of Veteran's Affairs
http://www.ptsd.va.gov

National Child Traumatic Stress Network
http://www.nctsn.org

Prolonged Exposure Therapy Online Training (PE Web)
http://pe.musc.edu/

Prolonged Exposure Therapy for PTSD training
http://www.med.upenn.edu/ctsa/workshops_ptsd.html

Richard Sears (author's website)
www.psych-insights.com

Richard Davidson (brain research)
richardjdavidson.com

SAMHSA's National Registry of Evidence-based Programs and Practices
http://nrepp.samhas.gov/

Susan Woods (MBSR/MBCT trainer)
www.slwoods.com

UCSD Center for Mindfulness, Mindfulness-Based Professional Training Institute
http://www.mbpti.org

UK Network for Mindfulness-Based Teacher Training Organisations
mindfulnessteachersuk.org.uk

References

Abbass, A. A., & Town, J. M. (2016). Bona Fide Psychotherapy Models Are Equally Effective for Major Depressive Disorder: Future Research Directions. *JAMA Psychiatry, 73*(9), 893-894. doi:10.1001/jamapsychiatry.2016.1916.

Ader, R., & Cohen, N. (1975). Behaviorally conditioned immunosuppression. *Psychosomatic Medicine, 37*(4), 333-340.

Albers, S. (2003). *Eating mindfully: How to end mindless eating and enjoy a balanced relationship with food.* Oakland, CA: New Harbinger Publications, Inc.

American Psychiatric Association. (2012). *Diagnostic and statistical manual of mental disorders* (5th ed.). Washington, DC: Author.

American Psychological Association. (2016). Stress in America: The impact of discrimination. Stress in America™ Survey. Retrieved from *http://www.apa.org/news/press/releases/stress/*

American Psychological Association. (2014). Stress in America: Are Teens Adopting Adults' Stress Habits? Stress in America™ Survey. Retrieved from *http://www.apa.org/news/press/releases/stress/*

American Psychological Association. (2012). Stress in America: Our Health Risk. Stress in America™ Survey. Retrieved from *http://www.apa.org/news/press/releases/stress/*

APA Division 12. (2016). Research-supported psychological treatments. Accessed April 17, 2016 from *www.psychologicaltreatments.org.*

Aronson, E. (2012). *The social animal* (11th ed.). New York: Worth Publishers.

Avey, H., Matheny, K. B., Robbins, A., & Jacobson, T. A. (2003). Health care providers' training, perceptions, and practices regarding stress and health outcomes. *Journal of the National Medical Association, 95*(9), 833, 836-845.

Ayton, P., & Fischer, I. (2004). The hot hand fallacy and the gambler's fallacy: Two faces of subjective randomness? *Memory & cognition, 32*(8), 1369-1378.

Barkley, R. A. (2013). *Defiant children: A clinician's manual for assessment and parent training.* New York: Guilford Press.

Baumrind, D. (1996). The Discipline Controversy Revisited. *Family Relations, 45*(4), 405–414. *http://doi.org/10.2307/585170*

Beck, A. T., Rush, A. J., Shaw, B. F., & Emery, G. (1979). *Cognitive therapy for depression.* New York: The Guilford Press, p. 11. ISBN 0-89862-919-5.

Beckman, H. B., Markakis, K. M., Suchman, A. L., & Frankel, R. M. (1994). The doctor-patient relationship and malpractice: Lessons from plaintiff depositions. *Archives of Internal Medicine, 154*(12), 1365-70.

Berila, B. (2014). Contemplating the effects of oppression: Integrating mindfulness into diversity classrooms. *The Journal of Contemplative Inquiry,1*(1).

Birnie, K., Speca, M., & Carlson, L. E. (2010). Exploring self-compassion and empathy in the context of mindfulness-based stress reduction (MBSR). *Stress and Health, 26,* 359–371.

Bowen, S., Chawla, N., & Marlatt, G. A. (2011). *Mindfulness-based relapse prevention for addictive behaviors: A clinician's guide*. New York: Guilford Press.

Burns, D. D. (1989). *The feeling good handbook*. New York: Plume.

Byerly-Lamm, K. (2017). *The Impact of Mindfulness-Based Cognitive Therapy (MBCT) on stress and affect in a community sample* (Unpublished doctoral dissertation). Union Institute & University, Cincinnati, Ohio.

Carson, J. W., Carson, K. M., Gil, K. M., & Baucom, D. H. (2004). Mindfulness-based relationship enhancement. *Behavior therapy, 35*(3), 471-494.

Carlson, N. R., & Birkett, M. A. (2017). *Physiology of behavior*. Boston: Pearson.

Chard, K. M. (2005). An evaluation of cognitive processing therapy for the treatment of posttraumatic stress disorder related to childhood sexual abuse. *Journal of Consulting and Clinical Psychology, 73*, 965-971.

Chu, J., Leino, A., Pflum, S., & Sue, S. (2016). A model for the theoretical basis of cultural competency to guide psychotherapy. *Professional Psychology: Research and Practice, 47*(1), 18.

Costa, P. & Widiger, T. (2002). *Personality disorders and the five-factor model of personality* (2nd ed.). Washington, DC: American Psychological Association.

Cotton, S., Luberto, C., Sears, R. W., Strawn, J., Wasson, R., & DelBello, M. (2015). Mindfulness-based cognitive therapy for youth with anxiety disorders at risk for bipolar disorder: A pilot trial. *Early Intervention in Psychiatry*. doi:10.1111/eip.12216.

Crane, R. (2009). *Mindfulness-based cognitive therapy*. London and New York: Routledge.

Dahl, J. A., & Lundgren, T. (2006). *Living beyond your pain: Using acceptance and commitment therapy to ease chronic pain*. Oakland, CA: New Harbinger Publications.

Davis, D., & Hayes, H. (2011). What are the benefits of mindfulness? A practice review of psychotherapy-related research. *Psychotherapy, 48*(2), 198–208. DOI: 10.1037/a0022062.

Davis, L. (2016). *Meditations for Healing Trauma: Mindfulness Skills to Relieve Post-Traumatic Stress*. Oakland, CA: New Harbinger.

Deckersbach, T., Hölzel, B., Eisner, L., Lazar, S., & Nierenberg, A. (2014). *Mindfulness-based cognitive therapy for bipolar disorder*. New York: Guilford Press.

Deslandes, A. C. (2015). Exercise and mental health: What did we learn in the last 20 years? *Progress in Physical activity and Exercise and Affective and Anxiety Disorders: Translational Studies, Perspectives and Future Directions*, 71.

Domjan, M. (2008). *The essentials of conditioning and learning* (3rd ed.). Belmont, CA: Wadsworth.

Duncan, B. L., Miller, S. D., Wampold, B. E., & Hubble, M. A. (2010). *The heart & soul of change: Delivering what works in therapy* (2nd ed.). Washington, DC: American Psychological Association.

Duncan, L., & Bardacke, N. (2010). Mindfulness-based childbirth and parenting education: Promoting family mindfulness during the perinatal period. *Journal of Child & Family Studies, 19*, 190–202. DOI 10.1007/s10826-009-9313-7.

El-Mallakh, R. S., Gao, Y., & Roberts, R. J. (2011). Tardive dysphoria: the role of long term antidepressant use in inducing chronic depression. *Medical Hypotheses, 76*(6), 769-773.

Ellis, A., & Grieger, R. (1977). *Handbook of rational-emotive therapy*. New York: Springer Publishing Company.

Ellis, A., & Harper, R. A. (1975). *A new guide to rational living*. Englewood Cliffs, NJ: Prentice-Hall.

Ferster, C. B., & Skinner, B. F. (1957). *Schedules of reinforcement*. New York: Appleton-Century-Crofts.

Fitzgerald, P. (2004). Repetitive transcranial magnetic stimulation and electroconvulsive therapy: Complementary or competitive therapeutic options in depression? *Australasian Psychiatry, 12*, 234–238.

Fletcher, L., & Hayes, S. C. (2005). Relational Frame Theory, Acceptance and Commitment Therapy, and a functional analytic definition of mindfulness. *Journal of Rational-Emotive and Cognitive-Behavioral Therapy, 23*(4), 315-336.

Foa, E. B., Hembree, E. A., & Rothbaum, B. O. (2007). *Prolonged exposure therapy for PTSD: Emotional processing of traumatic experiences: Therapist guide.* Oxford, UK: Oxford University Press.

Fouad, N., Gerstein, L., & Toporek, R. (2006). Social justice and counseling psychology in context. In R. Toporek, L. Gerstein, N. Fouad, G. Roysircar, & T. Israel (Eds.), *Handbook for social justice in counseling psychology.* Thousand Oaks, CA: Sage Publications.

Follette, V. M., Briere, J., Rozelle, D., Hopper, J. W., & Rome, D. I. (Eds.). (2015). *Mindfulness-oriented interventions for trauma: Integrating contemplative practices.* New York: The Guilford Press.

Frost, N. D., Laska, K. M., & Wampold, B. E. (2014). The evidence for present-centered therapy as a treatment for posttraumatic stress disorder. *Journal of Traumatic Stress, 27,* 1-8.

Fulton, P. (2005). Mindfulness as clinical training. In C. Germer, R. Siegel, & P. Fulton (Eds.), *Mindfulness and psychotherapy.* New York: Guilford Press.

Gallardo, M. E. (Ed.). (2014). *Developing cultural humility: Embracing race, privilege, and power.* Los Angeles, CA: Sage Publications.

Gershoff, E. T., & Grogan-Kaylor, A. (2016). Spanking and child outcomes: Old controversies and new meta-analyses. *Journal of Family Psychology, 30*(4), 453-469. http://dx.doi.org/10.1037/fam0000191.

Glasser, H., & Easley, J. (2013). *Transforming the difficult child: The nurtured heart approach — shifting the intense child to new patterns of success and strengthening all children on the inside.* Tucson, AZ: Howard Glasser.

Grepmair, L., Mietterlehner, F., Loew, T., Bachler, E., Rother, W., & Nickel, N. (2007). Promoting mindfulness in psychotherapists in training influences the treatment results of their patients: A randomized, double-blind, controlled study. *Psychotherapy and Psychosomatics, 76,* 332–338. doi:10.1159/000107560.

Hall, E. (1975). *From pigeons to people: A look at behavior shaping.* Boston: Houghton Mifflin.

Hanson, R., & Mendius, R. (2009). *Buddha's brain: The practical neuroscience of happiness, love & wisdom.* Oakland, CA: New Harbinger Publications.

Harris, R. (2009). *ACT with love: Stop struggling, reconcile differences, and strengthen your relationship with acceptance and commitment therapy.* Oakland, CA: New Harbinger.

Hayes, S. C. (2004). Acceptance and Commitment Therapy and the new behavior therapies: Mindfulness, acceptance, and relationship. In S. C. Hayes, V. M. Follete, & M. M. Linehan (Eds.), *Mindfulness and Acceptance* (pp. 1-29). New York: Guilford Press.

Hayes, S. C., Strosahl, K., & Wilson, K. G. (2012). *Acceptance and commitment therapy: The process and practice of mindful change.* New York: Guilford Press.

Hayes, S. K. (2013). *The complete ninja collection.* Valencia, CA: Black Belt Books, a division of Ohara Publications, Inc.

Hebb, D. O. (1949). *The Organization of Behavior.* New York: Wiley & Sons.

Hewer, M., & Linehan, M. M. (2015). Data 'salvation' for suicide research. *Association for Psychological Science Observer, 28*(7).

Hick, S. F., & Bien, T. (2008). *Mindfulness and the therapeutic relationship.* New York, NY: Guilford Press.

Hofmann, S., Sawyer, A., Witt, A., & Oh, D. (2010). The effect of mindfulness-based therapy on anxiety and depression: A meta-analytic review. *Journal of Consulting and Clinical Psychology, 78*(2), 169-83.

Hollis-Walker, L., & Colosimo, K. (2011). Mindfulness, self-compassion, and happiness in non-meditators: A theoretical and empirical examination. *Personality and Individual Differences, 50,* 222–227.

Hölzel, B., Lazar, S., Gard, T., Schuman-Olivier, Z., Vago, D., & Ott, U. (2011). How does mindfulness meditation work? Proposing mechanisms of action from a conceptual and neural perspective. *Perspectives on Psychological Science, 6* (6) 537-559. DOI: 10.1177/1745691611419671.

Huntington, B., & Kuhn, N. (2003). Communication gaffes: a root cause of malpractice claims. *Proceedings, Baylor University Medical Center, 16*(2), 157–161.

Isis, P. (2016). *The mindful doodle book: 75 creative exercises to help you live in the moment.* Eau Claire, WI: PESI Publishing & Media.

Jacobs, A. M., Hopton, J., Davies, D., Wright, N. P., Kelly, O. P., & Turkington, D. (2014). *Treating Psychosis: A Clinician's Guide to Integrating Acceptance and Commitment Therapy, Compassion-Focused Therapy, and Mindfulness Approaches within the Cognitive Behavioral Therapy Tradition.* Oakland, CA: New Harbinger Publications.

Kabat-Zinn, J. (1994). *Wherever you go, there you are: Mindfulness meditation in everyday life.* New York: Hyperion Books.

Kabat-Zinn, J. (2003). Mindfulness-based interventions in context: Past, present, and future. *Clinical Psychology: Science and Practice, 10*(2), 144-156.

Kabat-Zinn, J. (2010). *Mindfulness meditation for pain relief: Guided practices for reclaiming your body and your life* [audio CD]. Boulder, CO: Sounds True.

Kabat-Zinn, J. (2013). *Full catastrophe living: Using the wisdom of your body and mind to face stress, pain, and illness* (rev. ed.). New York: Bantam.

Keller, M., Lavori, P., Lewis, C., & Klerman, G. (1983). Predictors of relapse in major depressive disorder. *JAMA,* 250. 3299-3304.

Khan, A., & Brown, W. A. (2015). Antidepressants versus placebo in major depression: an overview. *World Psychiatry, 14*(3), 294-300.

King, A. P., Erickson, T. M., Giardino, N. D., Favorite, T., Rauch, S. M., Robinson, E., Kulkarni, M., & Liberzon, I. (2013). A pilot study of group mindfulness-based cognitive therapy (MBCT) for combat veterans with posttraumatic stress disorder (PTSD). *Depression and Anxiety, 30*(7), 638-645. doi:10.1002/da.22104.

Kito, S., Hasegawa, T., & Koga, Y. (2011). Neuroanatomical correlates of therapeutic efficacy of low-frequency right prefrontal transcranial magnetic stimulation in treatment-resistant depression. *Psychiatry and Clinical Neuroscience, 65,* 175–182.

Kok, B. E., Coffey, K. A., Cohn, M. A., Catalino, L. I., Vacharkulksemsuk, T., Algoe, S. B., ... & Fredrickson, B. L. (2013). How positive emotions build physical health perceived positive social connections account for the upward spiral between positive emotions and vagal tone. *Psychological science, 24*(7), 1123-1132.

Kraemer, K. M., Wasson, R., Lyle, K., Wu, G., Sears, R., Attari, M. & Cotton, S. (2015, October). *A Four Session Mindfulness Program for Improving Stress and Well-Being among College of Medicine Faculty.* Poster presentation at CENTILE International Conference to Promote Resilience, Empathy and Well-Being in Health Care Professions, Washington, DC.

Kristeller, J., & Bowman, A. (2015). *The joy of half a cookie: Using mindfulness to lose weight and end the struggle with food.* New York: Perigee.

Kristeller, J., & Wolever, R. (2011). Mindfulness-based eating awareness training for treating binge eating disorder: The conceptual foundation. *Eating Disorders, 19*(1), 49-61. DOI: 10.1080/10640266.2011.533605.

Kupfer, D. (1991). Long-term treatment of depression. *Journal of Clinical Psychiatry, 52 Suppl.* 28-34.

Kuyken, W., Byford, S., Byng, R., Dalgleish, T., Lewis, G., Taylor, R., Watkins, E., Hayes, R., Lanham, P., Kessler, D., Morant, N., & Evans, A. (2010). Study protocol for a randomized controlled trial comparing mindfulness-based cognitive therapy with maintenance anti-depressant treatment in the prevention of depressive relapse/recurrence: the PREVENT trial. *BMC Trials, 11*, 99. doi:10.1186/1745-6215-11-99.

Kuyken, W., Crane, R., & Dalgleish, T. (2012). Does mindfulness-based cognitive therapy prevent depressive relapse? *British Medical Journal, 345*, e7194. doi: 10.1136/bmj.e7194. Published online 9th November 2012.

Kuyken, W., Watkins, E., Holden, E., White, K., Taylor, R. S., Byford, S., . . . Dalgleish, T. (2010). How does mindfulness-based cognitive therapy work? *Behaviour Research and Therapy, 48* (11), 1105–1112.

Lazar, S. W., Kerr, C. E., Wasserman, R. H., Gray, J. R., Greve, D. N., Treadway, M. T., . . . Fischl, B. (2005). Meditation experience is associated with increased cortical thickness. *Neuroreport, 16*(17), 1893-1897.

Libet, B., Gleason, C. A., Wright, Jr, E. W., & Pearl, D. K. (1983). Time of conscious intention to act in relation to onset of cerebral activity (readiness-potential). *Brain, 106*, 623-642.

Linehan, M. (2015a). *DBT skills training handouts and worksheets*. New York: Guilford Press.

Linehan, M. (2015b). *Skills training manual for treating borderline personality disorder (2nd ed.)*. New York: Guilford Press.

Longmore, R., & Worrell, M. (2007). Do we need to challenge thoughts in cognitive behavior therapy? *Clinical Psychology Review, 27*, 173-187.

Luberto, C. M., Wasson, R. S., Kraemer, K. M., Sears, R. W., Hueber, C., & Cotton, S. (2017). Feasibility, acceptability, and preliminary effectiveness of a 4-week Mindfulness-Based Cognitive Therapy protocol for hospital employees. *Mindfulness*, 8(3), 1-10.

Luedtke, B., Davis, L., & Monson, C. (2015). Mindfulness-based cognitive-behavioral conjoint therapy for posttraumatic stress disorder: a case study. *Journal of Contemporary Psychotherapy, 45*(4), 227-234. doi:10.1007/s10879-015-9298-z.

Ma, S., & Teasdale, J. (2004). Mindfulness-based cognitive therapy for depression: Replication and exploration of differential relapse prevention effects. *Journal of Consulting and Clinical Psychology*, 72, 31-40.

Mårtensson, B., Pettersson, A., Berglund, L., & Ekselius, L. (2015). Bright white light therapy in depression: a critical review of the evidence. *Journal of affective disorders, 182*, 1-7.

Masuda, A. (Ed.). (2014). *Mindfulness and acceptance in multicultural competency: A contextual approach to sociocultural diversity in theory and practice*. Oakland, CA: New Harbinger Publications.

McAdams III, C. R., & Foster, V. A. (2000). Client suicide: Its frequency and impact on counselors. *Journal of Mental Health Counseling, 22*(2), 107.

McBee, L. (2008). *Mindfulness-based elder care: A CAM model for frail elders and their caregivers*. New York: Springer Pub.

McCown, D., Reibel, D., & Micozzi, M. S. (2011). *Teaching mindfulness: A practical guide for clinicians and educators*. New York: Springer.

McGrath, P. (2013, November). Taking Anxiety Disorder Treatment to the Next Level: Using Exposure and Response Prevention for Maximum Effect. 47th ABCT Annual Convention, Nashville, TN.

McLellan, A. T., Lewis, D. C., O'Brien, C. P., & Kleber, H. D. (2000). Drug dependence, a chronic medical illness: Implications for treatment, insurance, and outcomes evaluation. *JAMA, 284*(13), 1689-1695.

McMyler, C., & Pryjmachuk, S. (2008). Do 'no-suicide' contracts work?. *Journal of psychiatric and mental health nursing, 15*(6), 512-522.

Miller, M. (1985). *Information Center: Training workshop manual*. San Diego: Information Center.

Miller, W. R., & Rollnick, S. (2013). *Motivational interviewing: Helping people change* (3rd ed.). New York, NY: Guilford Press.

Miltenberger, R. (2012). *Behavior modification, principles and procedures* (5th ed., pp. 87-99). Wadsworth Publishing Company.

Mocking, R. J. T., Harmsen, I., Assies, J., Koeter, M. W. J., Ruhé, H. G., & Schene, A. H. (2016). Meta-analysis and meta-regression of omega-3 polyunsaturated fatty acid supplementation for major depressive disorder. *Translational psychiatry, 6*(3), e756.

Monson, C. M., & Fredman, S. J. (2012). *Cognitive-behavioral conjoint therapy for PTSD: Harnessing the healing power of relationships.* New York: Guilford Press.

Moreau, V., Rouleau, N., & Morin, C. M. (2013). Sleep, attention, and executive functioning in children with attention-deficit/hyperactivity disorder. *Archives of clinical neuropsychology, 28*(7), 692-699.

Morris, E. M. J., Johns, L. C., & Oliver, J. E. (Eds.). (2013). *Acceptance and Commitment Therapy and Mindfulness for Psychosis.* Hoboken, NJ: Wiley.

National Sleep Foundation. (2016). How much sleep do we really need? Retrieved from *http://www. sleepfoundation.org/article/how-sleep-works/how-much-sleep-do-we-really-need*

Neff, K. D. (2003). Self-compassion: An alternative conceptualization of a healthy attitude toward oneself. *Self and Identity, 2,* 85–101.

Padberg, F., & Moller, H. J. (2003). Repetitive transcranial magnetic stimulation: Does it have potential in the treatment of depression? *CNS Drugs, 17,* 383–403.

Pashler, H. E. (1998). *The psychology of attention.* Cambridge: MIT Press.

Pavlov, I. P. (1927). *Conditioned reflexes: An investigation of the physiological activity of the cerebral cortex* (G. V. Anrep, Trans.). New York: Dover.

Pederson, L. (2015). *Dialectical behavior therapy: A contemporary guide for practitioners.* Chichester, West Sussex, UK: Wiley-Blackwell.

Piaget, J. (1950). *The psychology of intelligence.* New York, NY: Harcourt Brace.

Piaget, J., & Morf, A. (1958). Les isomorphismes partiels entre les structures logiques et les structures perceptives. In J. Piaget (Ed.), *Etudes d'epistemologie genetique, Vol VI: Logique et perception* (pp. 52-166). Paris, France: Paris Presses Universitaires de France.

Piet, J., & Hougaard, E. (2011). The effect of mindfulness-based cognitive therapy for prevention of relapse in recurrent major depressive disorder: A systematic review and meta-analysis. *Clinical Psychology Review, 31,* 1032-1040.

Prochaska, J. O. (1999). How do people change, and how can we change to help many more people? In M. Hubble, B. Duncan, & S. Miller (Eds.), *The heart and soul of change: What works in therapy.* Washington, DC: American Psychological Association.

Prochaska, J. O., & DiClemente, C. C. (1992). The transtheoretical approach. In J. D. Norcross & M. R. Goldfried (Eds.), *Handbook of psychotherapy integration* (pp. 300-334). New York: Basic Books.

Prochaska, J. O., DiClemente, C. C., & Norcross, J. C. (1992). In search of how people change. *American Psychologist, 47,* 1102-1114.

Prochaska, J. O., & Norcross, J. C. (2010). *Systems of psychotherapy: A transtheoretical analysis* (7th edition). Pacific Grove, CA: Brooks/Cole.

Raine, A., Meloy, J. R., Bihrle, S., Stoddard, J., et al. (1998). Reduced prefrontal and increased subcortical brain functioning assessed using positron emission tomography in predatory and affective murderers. *Behavioral Science and the Law, 16,* 319–332.

Raine, A., Lencz, T., Bihrle, S., LaCasse, L., et al. (2000). Reduced Prefrontal Gray Matter Volume and Reduced Autonomic Activity in Antisocial Personality Disorder. *Archives of General Psychiatry, 57*(2), 119–127.

Reddy, S. (2016). The Best Temperature for a Good Night's Sleep: Light and time aren't as important as temperature, new research shows. *Wall Street Journal,* February 22.

Rescorla, R. A., & Heth, C. D. (1975). Reinstatement of fear to an extinguished conditioned stimulus. *Journal of Experimental Psychology: Animal Behavioral Processes, 1*(1), 88–96.

Resick, P. A., Galovski, T. E., Uhlmansiek, M., Scher, C. D., Clum, G. A., & Young-Xu, Y. (2008). A randomized clinical trial to dismantle components of cognitive processing therapy for posttraumatic stress disorder in female victims of interpersonal violence. *Journal of Consulting and Clinical Psychology,* 76, 243-258.

Reynolds, G. S. (1968). *A primer of operant conditioning.* Glenview, IL: Scott, Foresman.

Rosen, C. S., Greenbaum, M. A., Schnurr, P. P., Holmes, T. H., Brennan, P. L., & Friedman, M. J. (2013). Do benzodiazepines reduce the effectiveness of exposure therapy for posttraumatic stress disorder? *The Journal of Clinical Psychiatry, 74*(12), 1241-1248.

Rosenbaum, S., Tiedemann, A., Ward, P. B., Curtis, J., & Sherrington, C. (2015). Physical activity interventions: an essential component in recovery from mental illness. *British journal of sports medicine, 49*(24), 1544-1545.

Rosenzweig, S. (1936). Some implicit common factors in diverse methods of psychotherapy. *American Journal of Orthopsychiatry, 6*(3), 412–415.

Rudd, M. D., Mandrusiak, M., & Joiner Jr, T. E. (2006). The case against no-suicide contracts: The commitment to treatment statement as a practice alternative. *Journal of clinical psychology, 62*(2), 243-251.

Sapolsky, R. M. (2010). *Stress and your body* [audio CD]. Chantilly, VA: The Teaching Company.

Sapolsky, R. M. (2009). *Why zebras don't get ulcers.* New York: Times Books.

Sapolsky, R. M., Romero, L. M., & Munck, A. U. (2000). How do glucocorticoids influence stress responses? Integrating permissive, suppressive, stimulatory, and preparative actions. *Endocrine reviews, 21*(1), 55-89.

Schachter, S., & Singer, J. E. (1962). Cognitive, social, and psychological determinants of emotional state. *Psychological Review, 69,* 379–399.

Schnurr P. P., Friedman, M. J., Engel, C. C., Foa, E. B., Shea, M. T., Chow, B. K., ... & Turner, C. (2007). Cognitive behavioral therapy for posttraumatic stress disorder in women: A randomized controlled trial. *Journal of the American Medical Association, 297,* 820-830.

Schoenfeld, W. N. (1970). *The Theory of reinforcement schedules.* New York: Appleton-Century-Crofts.

Sears, R. (2015). *Building competence in mindfulness-based cognitive therapy: Transcripts and insights for working with stress, anxiety, depression, and other problems.* New York: Routledge.

Sears, R. W., Bruns, K., Cotton, S., DelBello, M. P., Strawn, J. R., Kraemer, K., Wasson, R., Norris, M., Weber, W. A., Durling, M. (2017). Neurofunctional changes associated with mindfulness-based cognitive therapy in mood dysregulated youth at risk for developing bipolar disorder. Paper submitted to the *Journal of Child & Adolescent Psychopharmacology.*

Sears, R., & Chard, K. (2016). *Mindfulness-based cognitive therapy for PTSD.* London, UK: Wiley-Blackwell.

Sears, R., Luberto, C., & Sell-Smith, J. (2016). Mindfulness-based approaches. In C. Haen & S. Aronson, *The handbook of child and adolescent group therapy.* New York: Routledge.

Sears, R., & Niblick, A. (Eds.). (2014). *Perspectives on spirituality and religion in psychotherapy.* Sarasota, FL: Professional Resource Press.

Sears, R., Rudisill, J., & Mason-Sears, C. (2006). *Consultation skills for mental health professionals.* New York: John Wiley & Sons.

Sears, R., Tirch, D., & Denton, R. (2011). *Mindfulness in clinical practice.* Sarasota, FL: Professional Resource Press.

Segal, Z., Bieling, P., Young, T., MacQueen, G., Cooke, R., Martin, L., Bloch, R., & Levitan, R. (2010). Antidepressant monotherapy versus sequential pharmacotherapy and mindfulness-based cognitive therapy, or placebo, for relapse prophylaxis in recurrent depression. *Archives of General Psychiatry, 67,* 1256-1264.

Segal, Z., Teasdale, J. & Williams, M. (2004). Mindfulness-Based cognitive therapy: Theoretical rationale and empirical status. In S. Hayes, V. Follete, & M. Linehan (Eds.), *Mindfulness and Acceptance* (pp. 45-65). New York: Guilford Press.

Segal, Z., Williams, M., & Teasdale, J. (2013). *Mindfulness-based cognitive therapy for depression* (2nd ed.). New York: Guilford Press.

Semple, R., & Lee, J. (2011). *Mindfulness-based cognitive therapy for anxious children.* Oakland, CA: New Harbinger Publications, Inc.

Shapiro, S. L., Astin, J. A., Bishop, S. R., & Cordova, M. (2005). Mindfulness-based stress reduction for health care professionals: Results from a randomized trial. *International Journal of Stress Management, 12,* 164–176.

Shapiro, S., Brown, K., & Biegel, G. (2007). Teaching self-care to caregivers: Effects of mindfulness-based stress reduction on the mental health of therapists in training. *Training and Education in Professional Psychology, 1,* 105–115.

Siegel, D. (2007). *The mindful brain: Reflection and attunement in the cultivation of well-being.* New York: W. W. Norton & Company.

Skinner, B. F. (1953). *Science and human behavior.* New York: Macmillan.

Skinner, B. F. (1969). *Contingencies of reinforcement: A theoretical analysis.* New York: Appleton-Century-Crofts.

Skinner, B. F. (1974). *About behaviorism.* New York: Knopf/Random House.

Smith, S. M., Fox, P. T., Miller, K. L., Glahn, D. C., Fox, P. M., Mackay, C. E., ... & Beckmann, C. F. (2009). Correspondence of the brain's functional architecture during activation and rest. *Proceedings of the National Academy of Sciences, 106*(31), 13040-13045.

Sohlberg, M. M., & Mateer, C. A. (1989). *Introduction to cognitive rehabilitation: Theory and practice.* New York: Guilford Press.

Sommers-Flanagan, J., & Sommers-Flanagan, R. (1995). Intake interviewing with suicidal patients: A systematic approach. *Professional Psychology: Research and Practice, 26*(1), 41.

Strawn, J., Cotton, S., Luberto, C., Patino, L., Stahl, L., Weber, W., Eliassen, J., Sears, R., & DelBello, M. (2016). Neurofunctional changes associated with mindfulness-based cognitive therapy in anxious youth at risk for developing bipolar disorder. *Journal of Child & Adolescent Psychopharmacology, 26*(4), 372–379. DOI: 10.1089/cap.2015.0054.

Sue, D. W. (2010). *Microaggressions in everyday life: Race, gender, and sexual orientation.* Hoboken, NJ: Wiley.

Sue, D. W., & Sue, D. (2016). *Counseling the culturally diverse: Theory and practice.* Hoboken, NJ: John Wiley & Sons, Inc.

Swallow, K. M., & Jiang, Y. V. (2013). Attentional load and attentional boost: A review of data and theory. *Frontiers in Psychology, 4.*

Tang, Y. Y., Hölzel, B. K., & Posner, M. I. (2015). The neuroscience of mindfulness meditation. *Nature Reviews Neuroscience, 16*(4), 213-225.

Teasdale, J., Segal, Z., & Williams, J. M. G. (1995). How does cognitive therapy prevent depressive relapse and why should attentional control (mindfulness) training help? *Behavioral Research and Therapy*, 33, 25-39.

Teasdale, J., Segal, Z., Williams, J. M. G., Ridgeway, V., Soulsby, J., & Lau, M. (2000). Prevention of relapse/recurrence in major depression by mindfulness-based cognitive therapy. *Journal of Consulting and Clinical Psychology*, 68, 615-623.

Torneke, N., Barnes-Holmes, D., & Hayes, S. C. (2010). *Learning RFT: An introduction to relational frame theory and its clinical applications*. Oakland, CA: Context Press.

Trower, P., Casey, A. & Dryden, W. (1998). *Cognitive-behavioural counselling in action*. London: Sage.

Ucros, G. (1989). Mood state-dependent memory: A meta-analysis. *Cognition & Emotion, 3*(2), 139-169. DOI: 10.1080/02699938908408077.

VanElzakker, M. B., Dahlgren, M. K., Davis, F. C., Dubois, S. & Shin, L. M. (2014). From Pavlov to PTSD: The extinction of conditioned fear in rodents, humans, and anxiety disorders. *Neurobiology of Learning and Memory, 113*, 3–18. doi:10.1016/j.nlm.2013.11.014 PMID 24321650.

Vestergaard-Poulsen, P., van Beek, M., Skewes, J., Bjarkam, C. R., Stubberup, M., Bertelsen, J., & Roepstorff, A. (2009). Long-term meditation is associated with increased gray matter density in the brain stem. *Neuroreport, 20*(2), 170-174.

Walser, R. D., & Westrup, D. (2007). *Acceptance & commitment therapy for the treatment of post-traumatic stress disorder & trauma-related problems: A practitioner's guide to using mindfulness & acceptance strategies*. Oakland, CA: New Harbinger Publications.

Walser, R. D., & Westrup, D. (2009). *The mindful couple: How acceptance and mindfulness can lead you to the love you want*. Oakland, CA: New Harbinger Publications.

Wampold, B. E., & Imel, Z. E. (2015). *The great psychotherapy debate: the evidence for what makes psychotherapy work* (2nd ed.). New York: Routledge.

Wansink, B. (2006). *Mindless eating: Why we eat more than we think*. New York: Bantam Books.

Watts, A. (1957). *The way of Zen*. New York: Pantheon.

Watts, A. (2004). *Learning the human game [audio CD]*. Louisville, CO: Sounds True.

Wexler, J., & Ott, B. D. (2006). *The relationship between therapist mindfulness and the therapeutic alliance*. Doctoral dissertation, Massachusetts School of Professional Psychology.

Whitaker, R. (2016). The case against psychiatric drugs. *Cadernos Brasileiros de Saúde Mental/Brazilian Journal of Mental Health, 8*(17), 1-16.

Whitaker, R., & Cosgrove, L. (2015). The End Product: Clinical Practice Guidelines. In *Psychiatry Under the Influence* (pp. 135-151). Palgrave Macmillan US.

Williams, J. M. G., & Kuyken, W. (2012). Mindfulness-based cognitive therapy: A promising new approach to preventing depressive relapse. *British Journal of Psychiatry, 200*, 359-360. doi: 10.1192/bjp.bp.111.104745.

Winnicott, D. W. (1964). *The child, the family, and the outside world*. Harmondsworth, England: Penguin Books.

Woods, S. (2013). Building a framework for mindful inquiry. *www.slwoods.com*

Yalom, I. D. (1980). *Existential psychotherapy*. New York: BasicBooks.

**For your convenience, purchasers can download and
print worksheets and handouts from www.pesi.com/sears**

Made in United States
North Haven, CT
28 July 2023

39628180R00102